Strategic Leadership in Digital Evidence

Strategic Leadership in Digital Evidence

What Executives Need to Know

Paul Reedy
Agency Operations Manager, Department of Forensic Sciences (DFS), District of Columbia, Washington, DC, USA

ELSEVIER

ACADEMIC PRESS
An imprint of Elsevier

Academic Press is an imprint of Elsevier
125 London Wall, London EC2Y 5AS, United Kingdom
525 B Street, Suite 1650, San Diego, CA 92101, United States
50 Hampshire Street, 5th Floor, Cambridge, MA 02139, United States
The Boulevard, Langford Lane, Kidlington, Oxford OX5 1GB, United Kingdom

Library of Congress Cataloging-in-Publication Data
A catalog record for this book is available from the Library of Congress

British Library Cataloguing-in-Publication Data
A catalogue record for this book is available from the British Library

ISBN: 978-0-12-819618-2

For information on all Academic Press publications
visit our website at https://www.elsevier.com/books-and-journals

Publisher: Stacy Masucci
Senior Acquisitions Editor: Elizabeth Brown
Editorial Project Manager: Joshua Mearns
Production Project Manager: Niranjan Bhaskaran
Senior Cover Designer: Matthew Limbert

Typeset by SPi Global, India

Dedication

Without the love and support of my family, Jacquie, Isabell and Irena, this book would not have been possible. Not only the support for the duration of the writing process but also for their support in the many years prior that allowed me to take advantage of the many opportunities that were put in my path. From humble beginnings as a bench analytical chemist in a small, multidisciplinary laboratory to the privilege of leading the forensic capability at the Australian Federal Police, to then moving to the United States to help start up the new concept of the District of Columbia, Department of Forensic Science. All of the major decisions were taken as a family with an attitude of you don't want to say 'I wish I had…'. It was never easy, but the love and support that we have for each other kept us all moving forward. I consider myself to be very fortunate.

I have been very fortunate also, not only for the opportunities with which I have been able to engage but also for the great people and leaders with whom I have worked. The challenge with acknowledging the help that one has along the way (no one can do it alone) is that some important people will not be mentioned. I have enjoyed working with almost everyone I have encountered in my work and studies, even those people who might think that I did not like them much. For people with whom I might have had a testy relationship along the way, I was always better for the interaction having learnt something from every encounter. In short, I can genuinely say that almost all (I am scientist by nature, so nothing is absolute) people with whom I have worked are genuinely interested in their work and are committed and dedicated to doing well in primarily serving the community.

Max Houck, whom I had met through our work with the organising committee for the triennial Interpol International Forensic Science Managers Symposium, suggested that I move to Washington, DC, to set up the Digital Evidence Unit for the DC Department of Forensic Sciences. We were captured by the idea of setting up a fully independent forensic laboratory, a nice idea while it lasted. We still believe in it.

James Robertson suggested to me that I might be interested in joining the Australian Federal Police to set up the Computer Forensic Team. One of the reasons for his interest is that I did not know a lot about it at the time, so I would not get caught up in the technical minutiae, and I would be free to look at the field with fresh eyes. He was right, I did not know a lot about it, and together, we created something pretty significant. I don't think that either of us would have been able to do it without the other. Although we barely knew each other at the time, we became very close friends and remain so even though we now live on opposite sides of the world.

Sandra Lambert was the manager of the new policy group in the Chief Minister's Department of the Government of the Australian Capital Territory. I wanted to work in central government as I wanted to understand how government made decisions. Being an outsider, I could not understand how certain decisions were arrived at. Sandra introduced me to whole of government policy making, and I probably learnt more from her in a short 3 years than I did in any other 3-year period, including while I was at university.

Peter Smith, my first, second and third supervisor early in my career while I was working as an analyst in clinical chemistry, toxicology and illicit drugs. One of the most valuable lessons that Peter taught me was to tell it like it is, even when people do not want to hear it. Like James, Peter is a lifelong friend.

Simon Walsh, who took the position of Manager Forensic Operations after I left the AFP, was a great support to me and all other members of the Forensic Science Division. He is highly intelligent and completed his PhD while working full time in a very demanding role. It is no surprise that he is as successful as he was and has gone on to be. I am sure there is much more for Simon in the future.

Lastly, I have had the great honour of working with so many senior colleagues; it would be impossible to mention them all. Mick Keelty was the commissioner of the AFP when I first began. It was his foresight in a number of spheres that lifted the capability and importance of the AFP to become a critical part of Australia's national security framework. This included the preparation of the AFP to deal with the, at the time, emerging terrorist threat, in recognition of unrest in South East Asia, by building not only AFP capability and capacity but also that of South East Asian nations so that they were able to manage the threat themselves. Just as importantly, Mick recognised the important role that unsworn AFP members could play in the AFP achieving its mission and worked to remove discriminatory structures and practices to enable the full commitment of unsworn people. From before he became commissioner, Tony Negus drove the technological advancement of the AFP so that it could both respond to threats law enforcement and national security posed by technology and also to take advantage of technology to achieve its goals. Andrew Colvin was one of the most people-centred leaders whom I have met. Although Andrew became commissioner after I had left, he always lived the same values that were seen as commissioner. He was tireless in his pursuit of equality and diversity, challenges that are difficult in the community at large, but especially so in law enforcement. Finally, I want to acknowledge Ramzi Jabbour, one of the smartest police officers I have encountered. Ramzi was able to articulate the detective's dilemma and engaged with me to seek solutions.

Contents

Introduction

1

'Grabbing a tiger by the tail'

The objective of this book is not to provide the answers to questions about digital evidence as, if that is what I set out to do, it would be obsolete by the time that it is printed. In this book, I have set out to guide leaders and managers who find themselves in the position of being responsible for a digital evidence capability but who may have had little opportunity to be previously engaged with the field.

From my personal and professional experience, the field of digital evidence is absolutely fascinating and caught my attention when I first became aware of it. Having studied biochemistry as an undergraduate, spent most of my career working in toxicology and illicit drug analysis, with a short, but not insignificant detour in science, technology and innovation policy, my career pathway did not automatically point me in the direction of digital evidence.

In 2002 an acquaintance at the time, Dr. James Robertson, one of a very small handful of international, elite leaders in forensic science, suggested that I might like to join him at the Australian Federal Police (AFP) to establish the Computer Forensic Team. James was the manager of scientific services at the time and had just been given responsibility for the Computer Forensic Team, which comprised, effectively, seven people, spread across the five main offices of the AFP. Up until that time the Computer Forensic Team was not a team at all, but a collection of individuals who reported to the local command. They had no budget and relied on their ability to beg, borrow or steal equipment, much of it surplus from other business areas, and resources to conduct their work. Tools were whatever they were able to get their hands on, were often downloaded from the Internet or were persuasive enough to convince someone with a budget allocation to purchase a professional tool. There were no standard operating procedures, nor consistency of practice between each office, nor, often, procedures agreed between colocated colleagues. Quality assurance was ad hoc at best. Most of the practitioners were police officers who had an interest in computers and were largely self-taught through reading and talking within the community of practice. On occasions a practitioner was able to engage in some training if a visiting expert came to town, who would then talk the other members through what he had learnt. And yes, 'he' as all of the team members were male. Over the following 8 years, the Computer Forensic Team grew from that original seven people to a team of 60. Yet, even with that many people and significantly reengineering the work process, the team could not keep up with the demand for digital forensic support for all of the agency's investigations.

The AFP that I joined was not the AFP that I applied to join. When I applied for the position in May 2002, the AFP was a relatively small organisation of around 2500 people and did not have a high public profile. The AFP was primarily concerned with

Strategic Leadership in Digital Evidence. https://doi.org/10.1016/B978-0-12-819618-2.00001-2

crimes committed in relation to the laws of the Commonwealth of Australia, with the police services of the states and the Northern Territory investigating those crimes that were committed against persons and interacting with the public. That changed on 12 October 2002 when two bombs were detonated in Bali, Indonesia, killing 202 people, including 88 Australians. On that day, Australia changed, the mission of the AFP changed, and the AFP's forensic science changed. Following the completion of my security clearance process, I commenced with the AFP just a few weeks after the bombs, and the organisation was scrambling. My direct superior was working full time on the forensic response to the bombs and spent most of his time in Indonesia.

Although I had no preconceived ideas about the field, which was still in its infancy as a discipline, this provided the opportunity to 'invent' computer forensics in a new shape and form without any preformed opinions. In a quick conversation with James, I was given a list of five goals, in no particular order:

1. Develop and write quality documentation including standard operating procedures to ensure consistency of practice between each of the offices.
2. Gain forensic accreditation under ISO 17025. This was additionally challenging as, at that time, there were no forensic accreditation guidelines for computer forensics under ISO 17025.
3. Create a budget.
4. Assess each of the existing team members.
5. Develop a working relationship, and delineate responsibilities, with the newly formed Australia High Technology Crime Centre that was also hosted by the AFP.

After that, it was up to me. The resulting digital evidence capability became a critical function of the AFP and one of the world's foremost digital evidence capabilities. Along the way, I was able to experience and observe some excellent leaders who informed my views on how to lead such a capability. Some of these observations will inform the following pages, both directly or indirectly. The ongoing success of the AFP's digital forensic capability that has continued long after I left can be attributed to the frameworks that were put in place, some of which were organisation wide and some specific to the team, with the overall objective of helping our people succeed. I was continually in awe of what our people could achieve in many and varied challenging circumstances. There were occasional missteps along the way, but, as a learning organisation, something could always be drawn from the missteps.

It was like grabbing a tiger by the tail.

Technology is a factor for all three parties to a criminal action, the perpetrator, the victim and the investigator. Each of the three parties has intentions to either commit a criminal act, protect themselves and their property or to investigate the criminal activity. To do so, each party will access and use extensions to their capability and capacity, such as technology, knowledge, skills, human assistance, social conventions and procedures and social and organisational structures, to act on their intentions. The technologies employed by perpetrators fall into two categories, those that assist in committing the action and those that assist to escape detection.

Criminals are notoriously early adopters of technology and will, therefore, avail themselves of advanced technologies. As the capability of criminals increases, the ability of law enforcement to investigate is decreased and in the position of having to catch up. That dynamic leads to a perpetual arms race between criminals and law enforcement. In jurisdictions in which crime is rampant, the advantages in technology, organisation, information and training that criminals have over law enforcement is excessive.

Information technology enables the performance of many social actions in electronic form, including communicating, entertainment and banking. The Internet is a place where people engage in the social practices in which they would in the physical world, practices such as work, play and social interactions. Importantly, I took the view that cybercrime cannot be considered to be a new crime, but is an extension of criminality that would be committed in the physical world. Criminal activities in the electronic world are largely similar to those of the physical world and, therefore, reflect crimes of the physical world including fraud, extortion, theft, harassment, vandalism, prostitution, child exploitation, human trafficking, drug trafficking, corruption, political extremism and terrorism.

Despite that similarity, there are additional complexities of cybercrime that include the distance between the victim and the perpetrator. Further, the victim, perpetrator and the evidence are often located in differing jurisdictions. Criminals also have access to greater abilities to obscure their conduct with the use of anonymising technology, such as false identity, data erasers, encryption and darknets. Criminal law and regulation usually lags well behind advances in technology. In addition, user privacy is a core objective of product makers' and service providers' business models and laws, especially in Western democracies that seek to protect civil liberties, can serve to inhibit the objectives of law enforcement when conducting an investigation.

To state the obvious, criminals on one side and law enforcement and crime targets on the other have conflicting objectives and seek to use technology to their own advantage. Criminals seek to exploit technology such as communications, data and information in its various forms and purposes, for illicit gain. Crime targets seek to use technology for legitimate financial benefit, protection and pleasure. Law enforcement seeks to exploit technology in the pursuit of justice. For all three groups, technology is used as an extension of other capabilities, capacity and resources to pursue their own objectives, to do what they intended to do anyway and to weaken those who are opposed to those objectives.

This book has drawn from many sources including personal and observed experience, numerous peer-reviewed publications and published (universally electronic) information sources. The attempt has been made to give fair representation to the wide range of views, but I have, as the reader might expect, offered my opinion and editorialised in many places.

In the past decade the field of digital evidence has expanded to meet the challenges from advances in smart technology, smartphone apps, implanted medical devices and malware. People with new skill sets in artificial intelligence and data science are joining the field, and digital investigation techniques and methods are being applied to crime analysis and intelligence. Digital forensic intelligence is becoming a priority in order to understand interjurisdictional criminal activity. Best practice guidelines were established over a decade ago but do not meet today's challenges of smart technology and those challenges that are yet to emerge. Some best practice guidelines do not address memory forensics, database forensics or network forensics, which have become routine investigative techniques.

Although it is important to the field to be able to demonstrate competence and provide confidence to stakeholders, best practices and automated tools are not the panacea for digital evidence. Each digital evidence case presents new challenges for which digital evidence practitioners should be problem solvers rather than technicians who follow a set procedure. The future digital evidence practitioner will need to be equipped with the knowledge and skills to address forensic questions in the presented case [1].

On behalf of the Organisation of Scientific Area Committees for Forensic Science, the task group on Digital/Multimedia Evidence prepared a document entitled a framework for harmonising forensic science practices and digital/multimedia evidence. The task group was commissioned to clarify how digital and multimedia evidence fits within forensic science and to the broader question of forensic science itself. It is noted that digital and multimedia evidence is unique among forensic disciplines as it serves investigative, procedural and scientific functions with the outcomes synthesised into expert opinions and conclusions.

Building on from the fundamental principle that every contact leaves a trace, the task group note that '[a trace] is any modification, subsequently observable, resulting from an event'. Forensic science addresses questions that are, potentially, in all disciplines: authentication, identification, classification, reconstruction and evaluation [2]. They arrived at the following definition of forensic science:

> *The systematic and coherent study of traces to address questions of authentication, identification, classification, reconstruction, and evaluation for a legal context.*

The term *systematic* refers to empirically supported research, controlled experiments and repeatable procedures applied to traces. The term *coherent* refers to logical reasoning and methodology. The term *legal context* refers to criminal, civil and regulatory functions, which also extends into human rights, employment, natural disasters and security matters.

Digital and multimedia evidence includes the following subdisciplines for which descriptions are provided: speaker recognition, facial identification, video/image technology and analysis and digital evidence.

A number of trends and themes are evolving across the digital landscape with digital meshing and smart machines becoming more prevalent in the lexicon. A digital mesh is a human-centred theme that refers to the collection of devices, information, apps, services, businesses and other people that exist around the individual. As the mesh evolves, all devices, computer and information resources, businesses and individuals will be interconnected. The interconnections are dynamic and flexible, changing throughout the day.

It is widely acknowledged that the challenges and practice of digital evidence continues to become more complex due to the increasingly sophisticated and complex consumer and business technology environment. At a technical level and predictably, the impact of cloud computing and the rapidly growing prevalence of Internet of Things continues to challenge forensic analysts and their employing organisations. More surprising is the acknowledgement of the impact of human factors and human fallibility in the practice of digital evidence that, seemingly, indicates a shift (or a further shift) away from the previous general, although not universal, belief that digital forensics is a fact-based discipline.

References

[1] E. Casey, Editorial: the broadening horizons of digital investigation, Digit. Investig. 21 (2017) 1–2.

[2] NIST, A Framework for Harmonizing Forensic Science Practices and Digital/Multimedia Evidence, National Institutes of Standards and Testing: Organization of Scientific Area Committees for Forensic Science, 2018. Retrieved from https://www.nist.gov/sites/default/files/documents/2018/01/10/osac_ts_0002.pdf.

The forensic model is dead

2

The codification of forensic science is its downfall

The thoughts that are expressed here result from the reflection of the many experiences over a long career in forensic science and what I think the future holds. They are informed by the many crises that were encountered along the way including investigational and operational challenges, but also the organisational, technological, policy and legal challenges that required major institutional responses and reaction to emerging issues that especially presented new challenges to the existent paradigms. This experience includes working in a small agency in a small jurisdiction; a major law enforcement agency with local, national and international remits; a central government agency with responsibility for whole of government policy including science and technology; working in multiple countries; and the usual national and international forums that one encounters along the way.[a]

Although I am truly grateful for these opportunities, my experience and ideas are perhaps more informed by the leaders with whom I have worked or observed at both close quarters and afar and especially by my own mistakes. The future is going to present new challenges that are not generally anticipated by the majority of people and for which no play book exists. As I write this, news has broken of major international actions taken that will change the dynamic of relationships between countries and regions, possibly impacting on strategic alliances, but the nature of the changes is unpredictable and unknown even to those with high expertise and insight. At a more direct level, 5G communications technology is rolling out around the world, but the impact is, again, unpredictable. 5G will introduce monumental leaps in increased bandwidth and in reduced latency. It is widely understood that high-definition movies will be conveniently downloadable in a matter of seconds, but the changes that have real impacts on the lives of people can only be guessed. These changes will, therefore, present new challenges to the digital evidence capabilities for organisations.

The changes will not take place instantaneously, but will occur in waves. Without being overly technical the communication networks in developed countries currently contain some 3G components even though 4G was introduced to the commercial market around 2010. When communications technology transitioned from 3G to 4G, many unanticipated changes resulted. For example, the explosion in social media was propelled by the improved technology to the point where it has now become ubiquitous and a major form of communication and influence, but it has also become weaponized. Netflix moved from a traditional pay per rental system to begin streaming in 2007 and Hulu began streaming on 2008. Whereas 4G has about two dozen technical functions, 5G will add around another two dozen to that total.

[a] For further information, please see my LinkedIn page.

Strategic Leadership in Digital Evidence. https://doi.org/10.1016/B978-0-12-819618-2.00002-4

I take the view that people are allowed to make mistakes as that is how they learn and how organisations learn. But don't make the same mistake twice! The subject of this book, *Strategic Leadership in Digital Evidence*, has a focus on leadership. The digital evidence examiners and experts with whom I have worked have almost always been very clever people who enjoy the challenge of the work, engaging with the ever changing science and technology with which they are presented and solving the puzzles that they encounter through their case work. These people are the ones who form the cadre of experts in the field and are typically dissimilar to those in the rest of the organisation for whim they might work for, whether it be an agency or company in law enforcement, justice, national security, finance, litigation or any other of the increasing range of companies that see a digital evidence capability as a core asset of the company.

The title of this chapter is *The Forensics Model is Dead*, which might seem provocative, but I believe that it is apt, albeit, maybe with the caveat 'or at least on life support'. It is certain that technological innovations introduced to the consumer and business markets will continue to challenge organisations. The digital evidence experts will be responsible for disentangling and systematically aggregating the multiple digital traces from a wide variety of data sources to develop a coherent chronology of events to articulate a narrative or, as I like to say, to give a voice to the data and elucidate the #datastories.

Following many well-documented miscarriages of justice (and missed investigational opportunities) in the previous century, the forensic science community established accreditation frameworks to define a minimum standard to which forensic science should be conducted and to provide stakeholders in the justice with a degree of confidence in the results of testing. The frameworks for the accreditation of forensic science have converged and evolved to primarily align to International Organisation for Standardisation's ISO 17025 the general requirements for the competence of testing and calibration laboratories. In many jurisdictions, accreditation to ISO 17025 for forensic science is mandatory or strongly encouraged for forensic science service providers, including organisations offering digital evidence and digital forensic services. There is considerable debate in the digital forensic community as to whether accreditation to ISO 17025 is the most suitable accreditation framework for digital evidence, or even if accreditation is suitable at all.[b] On my commencement with the Australian Federal Police in 2002, accreditation for the new digital forensic capability was one of my five priority strategic initiatives. By that stage, I already had some experience with accreditation in the physical forensic sciences, both in establishing an accreditation program and as an assessor for the original assessment and reassessment of service providers, and I had the opportunity to see what worked well, what did not work and some common pitfalls. The purpose of discussing it here is to look at it from a leadership perspective.

Although my colleagues at the time probably regarded me as a contrarian, or an accreditation heretic, when it came to accreditation, I was disturbed at what I saw

[b] This is discussed further under 'Quality Assurance'.

as poorly implemented accreditation programs. In my observation, it appeared that around 90% of forensic accreditation programs were poorly implemented with the following common mistakes made:

- The 'difficult' person within the organisation, i.e. the one who did not seem to fit in with any other area, was often appointed to the role of quality manager. Establishing and maintaining a quality system is a challenging job that requires excellent relationship skills as the quality manager must gain commitment of hearts and minds of the practising scientists, their supervisors and other managers to the quality process. These same practising scientists would rather be doing the day-to-day case work forensic science for which they spent a lot of time and effort (and spent a lot of money) gaining an education and undergone extensive training to do, i.e. sampling evidence, subjecting the samples to tests and interpreting the findings of those tests. Importantly, the quality manager is required to intervene sensitively when things potentially go wrong. In one extreme example, the Quality Manager response to a failed proficiency test was 'The proficiency test result was incorrect. Fix it'.
- In an effort to anticipate every scenario, quality manuals were generally far too big and bureaucratic. A consequence of the size was that the policies and procedures were often impossible for examiners to comply with, they presented an unbearable burden for annual review and updates and were inevitably self-contradictory.
- Procedures and methods were mind numbingly prescriptive that took all decision-making away from the scientists. To become a forensic scientist, a person does a 3–4 year degree, usually followed by a higher degree. The scientist then will spend up to a year in training before they are able to independently perform casework, then they must follow a set of prescriptive procedures. I am mindful of Steve Jobs who famously said 'It doesn't make sense to hire smart people and tell them what to do; we hire smart people so they can tell us what to do'.
- Quality assurance was implemented as a transactional overlay to which compliance was required rather than used to underpin a culture of pride that delivered high quality and efficient services.
- Resulting from the compliance approach, quality was seen as something to be done by a person or a group of people who carried the title 'Quality [person]' in their role description, rather than a necessary part of the culture of the organisation.

Accreditation is a minimum standard that an organisation is expected to meet in order to conduct testing to the general satisfaction of stakeholders and peers. Although meeting the standard of accreditation is not a trivial task involving a significant commitment of resources and the attention of leadership, accreditation really is the beginning of the exercise. The rhetoric of organisations, however, is suggestive of a belief that they have reached the pinnacle of achievement. More importantly, given the substantial investment that has been made in achieving accreditation, there is often a reluctance to significantly modify the framework and its supporting documentation once accreditation has been achieved.

The first forensic accreditation exercise in which I was involved was for a very small, multidisciplinary organisational division, comprising approximately 30 people, of which the forensic science represented approximately 25% of the entire division. In the belief that forensic accreditation was going to be too large an undertaking, the decision was taken to seek certification to ISO 9002 for quality management systems and from which ISO 17025 is derived. In hindsight, this was a very successful approach.

Most importantly, as ISO 9002 is for quality management systems, the leadership of the organisation, including all of the unit managers, took ownership and engaged in the process and became the leaders of quality within their units. Quality became part of the culture of the organisation and significantly, it was not offloaded to another team, especially one with 'Quality' in its name.

Having gained ISO 9002 certification, the organisation then proceeded to forensic accreditation which, by comparison, was a less onerous undertaking than tackling the ISO 9002 certification and far less onerous that trying to complete forensic accreditation in a single task. Importantly the culture of the organisation through all of its levels became inculcated with a ground-up commitment to quality. This commitment was reflected in the structure and integrity of the quality system, which was readily apparent and noted by the independent assessment team.

The Australian Federal Police was the first organisation in the world to gain accreditation for its digital forensic capability and the journey was not a simple one. I hold the view that forensic accreditation is a risk mitigation strategy, which is the approach that I took to its implementation. It is an efficient framework to address the significant risks encountered in forensic science, particularly in situations where mistakes can be made and the consequences of mistakes can be severe. These consequences can include miscarriages of justice for the falsely accused, poor assessment of potential investigational leads, damage to the brand of the home organisation and loss of confidence by the community and the elected leaders (the funders) of the capability.

As we were the first organisation to pursue digital forensic accreditation, before the journey could be commenced, forensic guidelines for ISO 17025 in the Australian context needed to be established. The guidelines were completed by a working party of stakeholders under the auspices of the national accreditation body.

One of the challenges for digital forensics accreditation within an organisation that has already been accredited is that the existent organisational policies, guidelines and protocols are written with physical evidence as part of the mindset. This can lead to inflexibility, often deliberate obstinacy, in the interpretation of the guidelines. A very simple example: a requirement is that each page much be numbered, in the format of 'Page x of y', with 'y' being the total number of pages. The requirement is present for the sound reason to ensure that the case file is complete and available to all parties to the case, with no evidence missing or withheld when audited. So, when applied to digital evidence, does a page refer to the hardcopy page of a report or to an Internet page if it is relevant? How is that page represented when a copy is provided to counsel in digital form, such as on a CD? Strict adherence by quality managers to existing quality policies can place unnecessarily difficult barriers to implementation of quality systems for digital evidence.

Further to the challenge outlined above, the nature of the substrate under analysis (the data) evolves and changes rapidly along with technological innovation as do the tools by which the data are analysed. There are around two to two and half million apps available on each of the Apple App Store and Google Play, with regular updates occurring frequently. Forensic tools are regularly updated for several purposes including the need to meet the challenges presented by new and updated apps, particularly those that frequently contain evidence pertinent to investigations, such as popular communications apps and increasingly, those apps supporting Internet of Things functions. Under the conventional, inflexible and obstinate interpretation of quality assurance guidelines, updated tools should be revalidated prior to use and validated in the context of the new and updated apps. The section under 'quality assurance' discusses this in more depth.

The point of this discussion is that the conventional and inflexible interpretation of the forensic science guidelines for ISO 17025, while it has met its original objectives to provide guidance to a minimum expected standard for the practice of forensic science, is doomed to fail forensic science badly if the guidelines do not become more flexible and responsive to innovation in forensic science. As new technology becomes available, not only in the digital evidence space but also in the development of technology for the rapid application of the physical sciences, the current conventional accreditation model will come under increased pressure. Clients, purchasers and funders of forensic services will increasingly seek justification for sending their testing requirements to a laboratory that is drowning in bureaucratic process with long turn around times, when they can get it done cheaper and more quickly in-house using off the shelf technology or by alternative private sector service providers who appear to provide an apparently acceptable quality of service. The real danger here is, having lost the purity argument based on cost and turn around time, the service requesters will place technology in the hands of untrained officers who do not have a scientific understanding of the underlying principles. Their evidence will comprise the production of a certificate stating to the effect 'the machine says…'.

The decision will then be up to the courts to determine whether or not the evidence is acceptable. Theoretically, criminal courts that operate under common law jurisdictions employ adversarial processes to get to the truth and test the reliability of the evidence. Further, jurisdictions and their courts are often referred to as 'Frye'[c] or 'Daubert'[d] jurisdictions, which provide a framework for determining the reliability of scientific evidence. Unfortunately, the court systems in various jurisdictions are not well equipped to discriminate between satisfactory and unsatisfactory science have been found to be inconsistent arbiters of scientific evidence reliability. The scientific reliability in forensic evidence is the already the subject of many, many learned papers and books and does not warrant further exploration here.

So, what is the solution? Scientific and technical evidence requires a framework by which reliability can be ascertained and a value assigned to the evidence through the judicial process. Reliability can only be achieved through a standard framework for decision making, and the most appropriate standard is ISO 17025. It is acknowledged that gaining accreditation to ISO 17025 requires a serious amount of work and

[c] Frye definition—a common-law rule of evidence where the results of scientific tests or procedures are admissible as evidence only when the tests or procedures have gained general acceptance in the particular field to which they belong.

[d] Daubert definition—the factors that may be considered in determining whether the methodology is valid are: (1) whether the theory or technique in question can be and has been tested; (2) whether it has been subjected to peer review and publication; (3) its known or potential error rate; (4) the existence and maintenance of standards controlling its operation; and (5) whether it has attracted widespread acceptance within a relevant scientific community.

it is a significant challenge, especially for small organisations. As indicated earlier the best process that I have encountered to begin the quality journey and to eventually meet this standard is to commence with ISO 9002 certification, i.e. a quality *management* system certification. It provides the framework and guidance that focus on the management processes and instills a quality culture in the workforce. Under such an implementation strategy, team leaders will have quality management as a priority initiative within their performance plan and they will bring their team along for the journey.

The quality manager provides a core consistency and format for organisational definitions. It is important that the quality manager is an influential and accomplished leader within the organisation and seen to be so. As mentioned above, a consistent error made by management teams has been to appoint the 'misfit', the person who they could not place anywhere else in the organisation or the person who has a history of workplace conflict, as the quality manager. That person is the exact opposite of what is needed. The quality manager must be a leader, someone who people want to work with. They need to understand the role of the quality system in the organisation, that is, as a risk mitigation strategy that enables the organisation to work towards its mission of efficiently producing scientific results with a high degree of confidence. The quality manager must be resilient (the job is hard) and be able to influence and persuade their peers, their fellow team leaders and executive, by developing a narrative that others will buy into and instill pride in the work. A narrative of compliance, which is just a form of coercion and intimidation, will not cut it, but result in a box-ticking exercise that does not instill a quality culture, and will irreparably damage the culture of the organisation. A quality system built on a culture of compliance is not sustainable and will eventually crash.

Once ISO 9002 certification has been achieved, the step to ISO 17025 accreditation is a relatively small step where the focus is then on the scientific integrity of the methods and processes employed. People will have a better understanding of the quality framework. Inevitably in forensic science and especially in digital evidence, there will be situations requiring deviation from the standard procedures, despite the procedures having been written in such a way to provide for flexibility. The principles instilled by the focus on quality management systems will provide the framework for staff to systematically research and make appropriate decisions and to account for those decisions when deviations are required.

In the interests of time and space I will not take this any further as the subject of quality leadership could be explored much further and has been the subject of many books and papers. To take the principles and practice of quality leadership in a forensic setting and expand on the themes outlined in this chapter, it requires a book of its own. But, in the meantime, I am happy to be contacted and to engage in further discussion.

Statistical survey

3

In order to begin to contemplate the challenges facing the management and examination of digital evidence, it is useful to understand the scale of the challenge. The scale is reflected in the numbers with which we are dealing. As we work our way through this volume, we will see that the field continues to change rapidly and unimaginably as new technologies become available. The growth in the user numbers of various technologies, the volume of data and the diversity of the technologies all present additional challenges to the digital evidence environment. The statistics listed in this section are just a sample of those that are available and point to the impact on the task of examining digital evidence, no matter in which context it is being applied (Table 1).

In the world today, there are 2.5 exabytes of data generated on daily basis with each human expected to generate 1.7 megabytes per second [1]. The total of global Internet protocol traffic from cloud data centres in 2018 was 10.6 zettabytes [2]. To add some perspective the number of words ever spoken by humans could be stored on 5 exabytes of data if, perhaps, stored as text and on 42 zettabytes of data if stored as audio. The entire collection of the US Library of Congress is estimated to hold 10 terabytes of data in all printed material and between 3 and 20 petabytes for all audio, video and digital materials.

The digital forensic market is expected to grow from $4.62B in 2017 to $9.68B by 2022, an annual compound growth rate of almost 16%. The anticipated market drivers are government regulations, the increasing frequency of cyber incidents experienced by businesses and the rapidly growing presence of Internet of Things applications and devices [3]. Business and personal transactional activities will continue to migrate to electronic processes with deals and agreements that are made over email and confidential data stored on personal address books and storage media. The banking, financial services and insurance sectors are expected to contribute a substantial proportion to the anticipated growth.

In 2019 there were 8.3 billion mobile phone subscribers worldwide [4] for a world population of 7.577 million people or, to put it another way, 104.4 mobile phone subscriptions per 100 people in the world. There were 4.4 billion smartphones in use representing a third of global mobile connections [5]. In some developed countries a significant proportion of the population are smartphone-only users having forgone the traditional fixed phone. Smartphones are used for voice calls (57%), data usage (33.5%) and SMS (6.5%) [6].

The smart phone market has experienced some changes over the past decade with some vendors disappearing and new vendors entering the market. Although the number of operating systems has not grown substantially, each vendor brings their own particular flavour to their offerings. Although it is difficult to obtain an accurate and consistent picture of mobile phone market vendor penetration; there are clear shifts occurring in the market. Most notable of the shifts is the increasing presence of Chinese smart phones (Fig. 1).

Strategic Leadership in Digital Evidence. https://doi.org/10.1016/B978-0-12-819618-2.00003-6

Table 1 Nomenclature and factors of number of bytes.

Unit	Multiple	Base 10 exponential	No. of bytes
Byte (B)	1	10^0	1 byte
Kilobyte (KB)	1000	10^3	1 thousand bytes
Megabyte (MB)	1,000,000	10^6	1 million bytes
Gigabyte (GB)	1,000,000,000	10^9	1 billion bytes
Terabyte (TB)	1,000,000,000,000	10^{12}	1 trillion bytes
Petabyte (PB)	1,000,000,000,000,000	10^{15}	1 quadrillion bytes
Exabyte (EB)	1,000,000,000,000,000,000	10^{18}	1 quintillion bytes
Zettabyte (ZB)	1,000,000,000,000,000,000,000	10^{21}	1 sextillion bytes
Yottabyte (YB)	1,000,000,000,000,000,000,000,000	10^{24}	1 septillion bytes

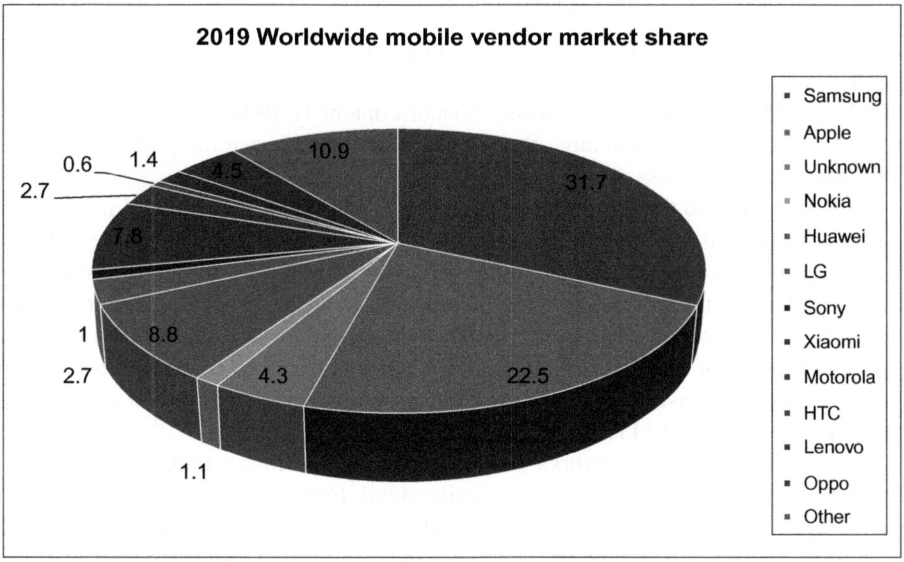

Fig. 1 Mobile vendor market share worldwide to September 2019 [7].

The worldwide spending on technology reached $3360 billion for 2019 and is expected to continue to grow year on year for the foreseeable future. Of that, 50% of the growth is in emerging technologies including Internet of Things software and hardware, augmented reality and virtual reality, software as a service and platform as a service, robotics, artificial intelligence, big data, data analytics and next-generation security [6]. Businesses are continuing to invest in new technology due to the end of life of legacy technology, to refresh existing capability, leverage new technology features and for software compatibility.

The major priority challenges for employers are to find workers with experience in emerging technologies, finding workers with so-called soft skills (i.e. interpersonal skills, ability to communicate in both oral and written form, ability to work as part of team, adaptability, problem solving skills, creativity, work ethic, time management, leadership and attention to detail). Although the description seems to be of the ideal employee, they are also the type of skilled workers that we will want to see in digital evidence. There is substantial competition not only between organisations but also between industries, for the right people to work in digital evidence in the government sector, whether that be in law enforcement, regulatory or intelligence agencies but also line agencies that see digital evidence as a necessary capability in meeting their mission.

The Internet is used by 58% (4.4 billion) of the world's population, a figure that is growing by 1 million new Internet users per day, with those users spending an average of nearly 7 h per day online. Within those Internet users, there are just under 4 billion active mobile Internet users. The activities in which Internet users are mostly engaged are video streaming, television content streaming, online gaming watching live streams of online games and watching e-sports.

In 2019 there were 3.5 billion users of social media of which almost 3.3 billion were mobile social media users. The most popular social media platforms are, unsurprisingly, Facebook, YouTube (owned by Alphabet Media, which also owns Google) and WhatsApp (owned by Facebook). Visual content is 40 times more likely to be shared on social media than any other type of media and hence the popularity of memes over text only messages.

When it comes to the compromise of cybersecurity, the consequential impact on a business or organisation can be devastating. The average cost of a malware attack to a business is $2.4 million, and the time impact of an attack is around 50 days. More than 90,000 websites are hacked on a daily basis with WordPress being by far the most targeted, with operational technology infrastructure compromised for 31% of companies. An average of 24,000 malicious mobile apps are blocked daily with a company falling victim to a ransomware attack every 14 s resulting in a total cost of ransomware estimated to be around $11.5 billion.

Fifth-generation (5G) networks were launched by mobile communications providers in the United States, South Korea, Switzerland, Finland and the United Kingdom during 2019. 5G is expected to be around 100 times faster than 4G and will be able to support millions of devices per square mile, which is a quantum shift from the current situation. It is anticipated that 7% of global communications service providers in 2020 will provide 5G services that will be able to make use of the 5G devices that manufacturers have released and that 5G phones will account for 51% of phone sales by 2023 [8].

In the foreseeable future the majority of businesses are planning to invest more in artificial intelligence and machine learning to improve business automation. This increase in spending builds on recent investments in machine learning, deep learning and natural language processing. The impact of these investments will mean that many business processes will be absent of human control. Further, there will be increased competition for artificial intelligence researchers, software developers, data scientists and user experience designers. The increased competition can be reasonably expected to impact on organisations that undertake digital evidence tasks and are seeking to build capability and capacity in this area.

With the increasing digitalisation of human experience, the growth in eCommerce will also impact on the demand for digital evidence services. Over 3.7 billion people engage in eCommerce. Further, it has become increasingly difficult to estimate the total and segmented transaction value due to the differences in functionality between FinTech (Finance Technology) systems used in, for example, alternative lending and assets under management in robo-advisors [9]. It is expected that there will be up to $4.8 trillion in transactions by digital payments in 2020 that substantially builds on an estimated 1.8 billion persons who purchased goods online in 2018 [10]. The challenge will continue to grow as spending on eCommerce is growing at over 11% per year.

The global market for Internet of Things devices is expanding rapidly. In 2016 it is was forecast that the IoT market would grow at a compound rate of around 35%, with an estimated 26.66 billion IoT devices in 2019 (which was very close to the forecast). It is further forecast that 8.3 billion IoT devices will ship in 2020 and reach a total of 75 billion installed IoT devices by 2025. Of these, there is expected to be 4 billion autonomous driving sensors by 2020 [4]. Within these figures, there are 3.46 billion IoT devices connected to mobile phones and 1.1 billion connected wearable devices [4]. Moreover, 40% of smart agents are expected to facilitate mobile interactions, and the postapp era will begin to dominate. Notably, 95% of cloud security failures will be the customer's fault.

Augmented reality (AR) is slowly becoming part of human's everyday lives through the use of AR glasses, AR training materials and for games. By the end of this year, it is estimated that there will be 1 billion AR users [11], with many media planning businesses intending to use augmented reality and virtual reality technology for their digital marketing campaigns. Augmented reality is becoming more accessible to citizens with mass-produced glasses costing less than $100 [12] and sales of glasses expected to reach 22.8 million units by 2022 [12].

Software as a service, which will be described in more depth later in this volume, is a software distribution model where the service provider hosts the application at a data centre, which can then be accessed by customers over the Internet. The SaaS model reduces costs for the customer as they will no longer need to maintain hardware and all that accompanies it. The global market in SaaS is expected to reach $157 billion in 2020 [13] and continue to grow for the foreseeable future.

As can be seen in the extraordinary growth and development in the various aspects of technology markets, including hardware, software and services, the impact on the management and examination of digital evidence will be ever changing and extraordinary. Digital evidence will continue to grow in both volume and complexity, but it will also grow in utility as the capability is applied to different situations and for different purposes.

Cybercrimes accounted for $2 trillion in global losses in 2019 representing, for scale, approximately 10% of the gross domestic product of the United States. Although small businesses pay little attention to cyberattacks, they are subjected of at least 50% of such attacks. It is expected that the estimated costs of damages will reach $6 trillion in 2021, which exceeds the global trade in illicit drugs. Further, it is estimated that a victim will fall to a ransomware attack every 14 s. The largest data breaches in history, where the personal details of account holders were the target, netted hackers hundreds of millions of accounts and, in one case, 3 billion accounts. Public organisations are estimated to receive one malicious email per 302 emails received [14].

References

[1] Domo, Data Never Sleeps, Retrieved from https://www.domo.com/solution/data-never-sleeps-6, 2019.

[2] S. Liu, Big data—statistics and facts, Underst. Stat. (October 1, 2019). Retrieved from https://www.statista.com/topics/1464/big-data/.

[3] Market Insider, Digital forensics market—global forecast to 2022, Retrieved from https://markets.businessinsider.com/news/stocks/digital-forensics-market-global-forecast-to-2022-1018885400, 16 March 2018.

[4] S. Liu, Internet of Things—Statistics & Facts, Retrieved from https://www.statista.com/topics/2637/internet-of-things/, October 24, 2019.

[5] S. Kemp, Digital 2019: Global Internet Use Accelerates. We Are Social, Retrieved from https://wearesocial.com/blog/2019/01/digital-2019-global-internet-use-accelerates, 30 January 2019.
[6] J. Chang, 150+ technology statistics you must know: 2019 & 2020 market share analysis & data, Finances (2020). Online. Retrieved from https://financesonline.com/technology-statistics/.
[7] Statcounter GlobalStats, Retrieved from. https://gs.statcounter.com/vendor-market-share/mobile, 19 October 2019.
[8] Gartner, Gartner says global device shipments will decline by 3% in 2019, Retrieved from https://www.gartner.com/en/newsroom/press-releases/2019-07-17-gartner-says-global-device-shipments-will-decline-3, 17 July 2019.
[9] Statistica, FinTech Worldwide, Retrieved from https://www.statista.com/outlook/295/100/fintech/worldwide, 2019.
[10] J. Clement, E-commerce worldwide – statistics and facts, Statistica (12 March 2019). Retrieved from https://www.statista.com/topics/871/online-shopping/.
[11] New Gen Apps, VR & AR statistics: shaping the future of augmented reality with data, Retrieved from https://www.newgenapps.com/blog/6-vr-and-ar-statistics-shaping-the-future-of-augmented-reality-with-data, January 1, 2018.
[12] A. Robertson, Leap motion designed a $100 augmented reality headset with super-powerful hand tracking, The Verge (April 9, 2018). Retrieved from https://www.theverge.com/2018/4/9/17208192/leap-motion-project-north-star-augmented-reality-headset-open-source-concept.
[13] S. Liu, Global public SaaS market size 2008–2020, Underst. Stat. (9 August 2019). Retrieved from https://www.statista.com/statistics/510333/worldwide-public-cloud-software-as-a-service/.
[14] M. Powell, 11 eye opening cybersecurity statistics for 2019, CPO Magazine (2020). Retrieved from https://www.cpomagazine.com/tech/11-eye-opening-cyber-security-statistics-for-2019/.

Definitions, disambiguation and differentiation of related fields

4

As one of the themes highlighted within this book, digital evidence is a rapidly evolving and changing field. The field can also be confusing with a wide range of terms used to describe what are essentially the same functions, and, often, one term has different meanings to different people. This chapter attempts to provide some clarity and distinction between the terms and the meanings.

Firstly, it is important to distinguish between the roles of the investigator from that of the digital forensic examiner. Much of the confusion has its roots in the history of the field when the then computer forensic functions were part of law enforcement investigation teams and were usually conducted by police officers who had an interest and proficiency (or familiarity) with computers. One of the pioneers in a major policing organisation related to me that he was asked to start doing the computer forensics as he was '…the one who knew how to hook up and switch on the printer'. In the early computer forensic models, the investigation and analysis of the computer was undertaken by the same person. In some organisations the computer was packaged at the crime scene and sent for analysis behind closed doors, and some months later a report was produced. As the field has evolved and the technologies where the evidence is located become more complex and sophisticated, the volume of data rapidly increased, and digital evidence has become ubiquitous in criminal investigations; there necessarily has been a separation in the roles.

To draw an analogy an investigation might encounter some documents in a filing cabinet that are considered to be of evidentiary value. The investigator might ask the document examiner to examine and report on the handwriting, the type face, the ink that has been used for printing and writing, any alterations that have been made and the type of paper. Further, some reference samples might have been provided by the investigator for comparison. The document examiner, however, is not asked to report on the content of the document and the meaning of the text, nor, if applicable, the nature of any transactions that might have been described in the text. That is the role of the investigator.

Many of the terms are used interchangeably, whereas each term has a specific meaning and should be used precisely and accurately. It is helpful to define the scope of various terms used within and related to digital evidence.

API (application programming interface)

A set of functions and procedures that allow the creation of applications which access the features or data of an operating system, application or other service and allow third parties to use the functionality of that software application.

Strategic Leadership in Digital Evidence. https://doi.org/10.1016/B978-0-12-819618-2.00004-8

APK

Android application package used by the Android operating for the distribution of mobile apps, mobile games and middleware.

Botnet

A botnet-infected computer (referred to as a 'zombie') can receive commands and be controlled by another party. A large number of zombies can be used to perform a distributed denial of service attack against a target that will significantly reduce its availability to customers.

Cloud computing

The National Institute for Standards and Technology define cloud computing as '...a model for enabling ubiquitous, convenient, on-demand network access to a shared pool of configurable computing resources...'. [1]

Computer forensics

The term 'computer forensics', although still used infrequently, is a largely outdated reference. Although conceptually similar to digital forensics, computer forensics specifically refers to computers. The term is outdated as computers (personal computers and notebooks) are outsold by other devices (mobile phones and ultramobiles) by more than ten to one [2], and an increasing proportion of digital evidence is located in cloud storage and IoT devices.

Cybercrime (e-crime or electronic crime, high-tech crime, computer crime)

Cybercrime (also referred to as cyber-crime and cybercrime) is perhaps the most flexibly used term in law enforcement, with many organisations choosing to define it specifically to themselves. Cybercrime is a crime in which a computer is the object of the crime or is used to commit a crime [3, 4]. An alternative definition for cybercrime is criminal activity that is committed using a computer [5]. Cybercrime may also be referred to as computer crime although, for similar reason to that listed in the preceding text, this is becoming an outdated concept. Conversely, despite the priority attention and resources that it devotes to a range of 'cybercrime' initiatives and functions, the FBI does not offer a definition of cybercrime. The US Department of Justice defines cybercrime through the description of three categories for crimes in which a computing device is the target, the weapon or an accessory. In common law jurisdictions, a criminal act comprises two elements–*actus reus* (the physical element or wrongful conduct) and *mens rea* (the mental element or knowledge of the wrongfulness of the act).

Cyberterrorism

The convergence of terrorism and cyberspace in which unlawful attacks and threats against computers, networks and the information contained within, in pursuit of political or social objectives. Cyberterrorism results in harm to persons or property, including to generate fear [6]. Cyberterrorism is one of many security risks faced by law enforcement. Although the likelihood of a kinetic or explosive attack delivered via the Internet is low, other applications are more likely and potentially useful to extremists. Examples of such applications include recruitment, radicalization, funding and organising attacks. The probability of a cyberattack causing a high-impact event, such as shutting down an entity of critical infrastructure, for example, an electricity service, remains low.

The distinction between cyberterrorism and cybercrime is based on motive, which might not always be easily discernible. For example, a terrorist group seeking to raise funds might perpetrate a crime to obtain funds, such as a fraud or ransom ware attack, whereas a business competitor might conduct a distributed denial of service attack that appears as a terror lionized attack, to gain a competitive advantage.

Cyberwarfare

The use of technology to attack a national is causing harm that is comparable with kinetic warfare. Cyberwarfare results in damage caused by cyberattacks that cause physical damage to people and things in the real world [7]. Cyberwarfare supports conventional military strategy, and the targets are usually selected for the damage to rival or enemy states' military and economic resources, especially communications. The distinctions are becoming increasingly blurred with comingling of terrorist and criminal activities with the tactical and strategic goals of nation states or quasi-state actors. Cyberterrorism is a form of cyberwarfare and is now the fifth domain of war, along with land, sea, air and space.

I propose the definition of cyber crime as crime in which data is the target, the weapon, or an accessory of criminal conduct. In arriving at this definition, it is the data that is the thing of value which is critical to crime and the ensuing investigation. As the complexity of technology and the greater range of devices, including IoT, and storage systems, a definition based on a physical entity has become less relevant.

Cyberweapon

There is ambiguity around the definition of a cyberweapon and debate as to whether it is suitable term to use for code that is used for malicious purposes [8]. The distinguishing feature is dependent on two psychological element. The first is of intent and whether or not it is intended to cause harm. For example, a hammer is commonly regarded as a tool, but if its use is to cause harm, then it becomes a weapon. Secondly, it must be perceived as a weapon. The same logic can be applied to malware. A cyberweapon is having three components: propagation, an exploit and a payload. A weapon is determined by whether or not the payload has the ability to cause damage to either the device or the data. This model is due to the potential for alternative uses of the other components of the weapon, that is, the propagation and the exploit [9].

Digital evidence

Digital evidence is information that is stored or transmitted in binary form that might be used as probative evidence in judicial proceedings, whether they be criminal, civil, administrative or political [10]. The evidence can be stored in any location and in an increasing range of devices and systems. An alternative definition of digital evidence that is, perhaps, more useful refers to a repository of electronic data that can be accessed. As the utility of digital evidence becomes more pervasive and is used in wider contexts that are not necessarily used in judicial proceedings, the second definition provides additional scope [11]. Yet, the second definition remains incomplete as it appears to exclude evidence that is stored on optical media, yet is still in binary form. Taking the above into consideration, we shall define digital evidence that is stored or transmitted in binary form.

Digital exploitation

Digital exploitation has a range of meanings depending on the context in which it is being used. It refers to the exploitation of a software vulnerability in the cybersecurity context. It can also refer to the extraction, translation and analysis of physical and digital documents and media to generate information.

Digital forensics

The National Institute of Standards and Technology refers to digital forensics as '...the field of forensic science that is concerned with retrieving, storing and analysing electronic data that can be useful in criminal investigations...'. [10] Again, in addition to the similarity and therefore the related concerns of this definition to the above text for 'digital evidence', the NIST definition implies the inclusion of electronic data that might be present in analog form, such as an analogue tape recording, or that data stored on optical media such as CD/DVD.Blu-ray. Further, digital forensics can be applied to other situations such as civil litigation and in cybersecurity investigations that are not necessarily criminal in nature. Notwithstanding the variance in definitions, the steps remain broadly the same. The traditional articulation of the steps in the digital forensics process are typically

1. identify,
2. preserve,
3. analyse,
4. report,

which remains a valid expression of the phases of the digital evidence process.

Electronic evidence

Many organisations and people working within the field use the term 'electronic evidence' interchangeably with some of the other terms described here. It is noted that the term 'electronic evidence' often appears in legislation and other legal references when the term 'digital evidence' will more precisely describe the subject matter. The term 'digital', as in digital evidence, refers to data represented in binary form but does not include analog records such as analog audio and video tape. Electronic evidence include both digital and analog forms or records.

Hacking

The gaining of unauthorised access to data in a system or computer.

Hacktivism

The blending of the terms activism and hacking emerged in the 1980s and has since steadily increased in prevalence. Hacktivism has increased in severity from online messages of protest to cyberattacks, web defacement, distributed denial of service attacks and hijacking of government websites. Hacktivist groups now include a broad spectrum of actors from loosely formed groups such as *Anonymous* through to some with associations to government agencies or are unaffiliated 'patriot hackers' and state-sponsored hackers. They represent a significant threat as they can impact popular opinion and create opportunities for disseminating false information [12].

Internet of things

A global distributed network connecting physical objects that are capable of sensing or acting on their environment and are able to communicate with each other, other machines or computers.

Logic bombs

Logic bombs execute under specific conditions such as a specific date or time. They might delete files, damage networks or release a virus.

NAND flash memory

Solid-state nonvolatile computer memory storage medium that is usually present in memory cards and USB flash drives. It is often used to store configuration data in digital devices such as computers, digital audio players, digital cameras, mobile phones, scientific instruments, industrial robotics and medical electronics.

RAM (random access memory)

A form of computing memory can be read and changed in any order. RAM allows data to be written or read no matter where it is located within the memory, unlike other forms of memory.

Rootkit

A rootkit is an application or set of applications that can disguise itself as a piece of software on a computer's operating system and can contain malware within its application. Rootkits are often used in the forensic examination of Android mobile devices.

SCADA

Supervisory control and data acquisition refers to the control architecture systems that are connected to peripheral or edge devices such as sensors and controllers that are employed in high-level process management for process plants, machinery and infrastructure.

Slack space

The space between the end of the file and the end of the disk cluster where it is stored. Slack space occurs because data rarely fills the fixed storage locations exactly.

Static analysis

The traditional type of forensic investigation is conducted on data at rest, such as the contents of a hard drive or flash drive.

Technology enabled crime

Technology enabled crime refers to acts that use, rather than attack, computers. Computers and the information contained within, or accessed, are the object of the criminal activity.

Viruses and worms

Viruses are programs that are able to infect other programs by modifying them to include a copy, or near copy, of itself. They replicate and spread to other programs, files and computers, and have the potential to alter, delete or corrupt data. Viruses generally require user interaction to execute. Worms operate similarly but can propagate by exploiting vulnerabilities in the machine's software or operating system.

Zero day exploits

A zero day exploit is a vulnerability in software that is unknown to the vendor or the user. It can be exploited prior to the vendor becoming aware and patching it.

References

[1] NIST, The NIST Definition of Cloud Computing, National Institute of Standards and Technology: Computer Security Resource Center, 2011. Retrieved from https://csrc.nist.gov/publications/detail/sp/800-145/final.

[2] Gartner, Gartner says global device shipments will decline by 3% in 2019, Retrieved from https://www.gartner.com/en/newsroom/press-releases/2019-07-17-gartner-says-global-device-shipments-will-decline-3, 17 July 2019.

[3] Techopedia, Cybercrime, Retrieved from https://www.techopedia.com/definition/2387/cybercrime, 2020.

[4] Australian Federal Police, Cyber Crime, Retrieved from https://www.afp.gov.au/what-we-do/crime-types/cyber-crime, 2020.

[5] Merriam-Webster, Cybercrime, Retrieved from https://www.merriam-webster.com/dictionary/cybercrime, 2020.

[6] D. Denning, Cyberterrorism: Testimony Before the Special Oversight Panel on Terrorism Committee on Armed Services, U.S. House of Representatives, 2000.

[7] P. Singer, Cybersecurity and Cyberwar: What Everyone Needs to Know, Oxford University Press, New York, 2014.
[8] T. Rid, P. McBurney, Cyber-weapons, RUSI J. 157 (1) (2012) 6–13.
[9] T. Herr, P. Rosenzweig, Cyber weapons & export control: incorporating dual use with the PrEP model, J. Natl. Sec. Law Pol. 8 (2) (2016).
[10] NIST, Digital Evidence: What is Digital Forensics, Retrieved from https://www.nist.gov/topics/digital-evidence, 2020.
[11] L. Daniel, L. Daniel, Digital Forensics for Legal Professionals, Syngress Publishing, 2012.
[12] D. Denning, The rise of hacktivism, Georget. J. Int. Aff. (2015). September 8. Retrieved from https://www.georgetownjournalofinternationalaffairs.org/online-edition/the-rise-of-hacktivism.

Digital forensics process

5

Facilitated by increasing storage capacities and the falling prices of storage devices, the exponentially growing volume of data is regarded by many commentators as the single greatest challenge to digital evidence. These observations are supported by Moore's Law (the number of transistors on an integrated circuit doubling every 18–24 months) and Kryder's Law (storage capacity doubles every 12 months), which, inferentially, means there is an ever widening gap between the generation of stored data and the ability to process it [1]. Consequently, there are substantial cost implications to the storage and management of the entirety of the seized data. The cost implications can be balanced against the benefits to be gained from comparisons between cases if the data are stored on a networked solution if the data are accessible for operational information and intelligence purposes.

Organisations, especially those whose core business involves investigations, are very aware of the volume of data that they will receive in relation to an investigation and the time that is required (as a general rule of thumb, an average, yet comprehensive digital forensic examination will take about 2 weeks, but an individual case can vary between a few hours to several months) to conduct an effective, comprehensive digital evidence examination. In conflict with the time and effort that is required, decision-makers are more frequently seeking increasingly timely responses to questions regarding investigations, perhaps due to the increased public and political scrutiny to which investigations are subjected. These conflicts are occurring at the same time that technological innovations are driving the growth in data volume and complexity. Consequently the discipline of digital forensics is under increasing pressure to conduct forensic examinations in a more focused, which infers a less comprehensive, manner. Considerable research into new approaches and potential new tools has been undertaken to hasten the examination process and to improve efficiency. Compounding that conflict is the relatively recently identified issue of cognitive bias and its probable impact on digital evidence examinations (addressed elsewhere in this text). Cognitive bias, if steps have not been taken to mitigate its impact, has been found to potentially impact the objectivity of forensic scientists when testing and interpreting case work. It should be noted that context bias impacts many human endeavours and is not restricted to forensic scientists alone. Research into the impact of cognitive bias in forensic science has led to the suggestion that, when conducting forensic analysis, the information provided to forensic scientists should be restricted to that which is task or contextually. Meanwhile, organisations are increasing demand to link similar or related activities using distinctive digital traces, particularly for the purpose of international intelligence, which will provide richer context for the digital forensic examiner. Most proposed methods for expediting the digital evidence examination process are based on the assumption that relevant information will be found in similar locations where it has been found in other cases. Consequently, evidence stored in previously unknown or new locations will be

Strategic Leadership in Digital Evidence. https://doi.org/10.1016/B978-0-12-819618-2.00005-X

ignored, which disregards two well-known features of the field: (1) New technology is regularly appearing in the market, and (2) criminal behaviour constantly evolves, and criminals are notoriously earlier adopters of technology.

The activities that are undertaken by the digital forensic examiner in the course of casework examination are the following:

- survey including the acts of searching, finding, detecting and recognising traces on sources of evidence, whether they are devices or accounts held in other locations;
- preservation of the digital traces to prevent any alteration;
- examination to observe the traces and their characteristics and to recover the information and content;
- documentation to record traces with associated context characteristics, forensic activities and provenance information;
- analysis to obtain more information about the characteristics if the digital traces and to make the results available for integration, classification, reconstruction and evaluation or interpretation;
- integration to combine the results of multiple analysis processes in order to obtain a more comprehensive understanding of the traces;
- interpretation to explain the meaning of forensic findings to reach well founded and informed decisions.

One approach to improving the digital forensic process has been developed by a National Institute of Standard and Technology task group. The document, *A Framework for Harmonising Forensic Science Practices and Digital/Multimedia Evidence,* identifies the core forensic processes that apply to all forensic disciplines including digital and multimedia evidence [2]. The core processes are the following:

- Authentication is the decision process that attempts to establish sufficient confidence in the truth of a claim. Authentication is also used in the identification, classification, reconstruction and evaluation phases to support the establishment of confidence.
- Identification is the decision process that attempts to establish sufficient confidence that some identity-related information describes a specific entity in a given context, at a certain time [3]. Identification is applied to not only human beings but also animate or inanimate entities, whether they be physical or virtual. Identification is also used in the authentication, classification and evaluation phases.
- Classification is the process of developing taxonomies of traces and ascribing a trace on the basis that characteristics are common among traces of the same class.
- Reconstruction is the process of organising traces to disclose the most likely operational conditions or capabilities, patterns in time and linkages between entities. Reconstruction can be a subprocess within authentication, identification, classification and evaluation.
- Evaluation produces a value that can be fed into a decision process. The evaluation process precedes every decision in the forensic life cycle.

Several approaches to mitigate the unmet demand for digital forensics, the impact of the rapidly growing ocean of data and the associated complexity have been developed and trialled around the world. One such approach involved conducting triage in the field by persons who were not digital evidence specialists. Crime scene investigators were trained in the field triage process, thereby reducing the time-consuming need for specialists to attend crime scenes. The frontline personnel received basic training in digital forensic analysis focused on ensuring the integrity of the digital evidence. The enhanced capability is an extension of a previous initiative in which crime scene personnel are trained to lift fingerprints from a crime scene, but they are not expected to conduct the fingerprint comparison function. Training and deploying crime scene personnel significantly improved investigational efficiency as investigators received actionable information in a timely manner that, in turn, then led to faster justice system outcomes to the benefit of all justice system stakeholders. However, caution and thorough planning should exercised before such a process is implemented as the question of 'sufficiency of examination' remained unanswered for which a more in-depth forensic examination and further research is required [4].

Noting that data on mobile devices are easy to modify but difficult to acquire in a forensically sound manner, the integrity of data can be reasonably assured by following standard procedures and best practices. One possible multidisciplinary digital forensic investigation approach for mobile smart devices builds on three subfields in the digital forensics domain: smart device forensics, network forensics and cloud forensics. The objective of the model is to guide the forensic examiner through the execution of a digital investigation that is compliant with the applicable laws, up to date and efficient in addressing the information technology. The process ensures that the traditional digital forensic process is followed from incident detection, securing the crime scene (the device) and making an initial assessment. The forensic examiner is then engaged to perform the preservation, and, if appropriate, any physical evidence obtained. The digital evidence is then acquired, examined, any links to external sources of potential digital traces identified and analysis conducted. The exception though is that an iterative process might be required therefore, following analysis, revisiting the preservation phase and ensuing phases might reveal additional evidence [5, 6].

Another approach to the examination of digital evidence has been inspired by concern over the near-blind trust that practitioners place in commercial systems and therefore they neglect to verify the production of the analytical results. This approach addresses the situation that is present in many digital forensic facilities where the examiner has increasingly become a passive tool operator who is more detached from the methods used to process the evidence. The new approach employs a standard query interface, or domain specific language, that enables domain experts to use a formal specification of the digital evidence process for the computation to be performed. The system architecture relieves the requirement to specify the computation to be conducted, instead of mapping it to the tools and scheduling it with the resources that are available. The architecture is agnostic thereby allowing for a range of tools to be incorporated into the system. Examiners can construct an analytical strategy using the range of tools that have been incorporated by constructing queries that are specific to the case under investigation. In using such an approach, big data and artificial intelligence techniques can also be incorporated into the architecture and applied to the case. Such an architecture could also be used to facilitate tool testing, tool validation and cross-tool integration [7].

The potential extension of such an architecture leads one to consider the opportunity for automation in the digital forensics process, such as the possibilities for robotic automation. Robotic process automation is the automation of service tasks that were previously performed by humans, i.e. technology that is based on the concept of artificial intelligence. Robot perform tasks according to instructions that are directed by the developer who communicates with the systems and then triggers the response to produce results. Robotic process automation is a higher level automation in which a software-based task that can be procedurally replicated and directed to perform the same sequence of software interactions that are required to complete the task. The robotic process automation core function interacts with the presentation layer of software, i.e. that which is visible to humans [8].

Robotic process automation has a number of benefits including lower cost and less time to implement, little to no disruption to underlying systems as it operates at the human level on top of existing software solutions, rather than being integrated with those same solutions. The benefits of using robotic process automation include (1) improved accuracy as it is less prone to procedural (human) errors; (2) improved employee morale as less time is spent doing the routine and mundane tasks; (3) improved productivity as the robot process cycle is much faster than manual processes; (4) improved reliability and consistency as robots can only carry preprogrammed commands and, therefore, perform the same way every time; (5) reduced risk to system damage as it noninvasive to underlying IT systems; (6) assured compliance with regulations and policies as requirements are preprogrammed in the robot, from which the robot cannot deviate; and (7) low technical barrier to implementation as no programming knowledge is required to configure a software robot. Automated processes are especially useful for the preprocessing tasks in the digital forensics domain. The subjective investigative tasks comprising analysis and interpretation of results are not suitable for automation as they are dynamic, instinctive and are influenced by specific circumstances of each unique case.

File carving is a long established, automated method for reducing the volume of data to be analysed in a given case. It involves the removal of superfluous, nonuser generated data, such as operating system files, etc., that are usually of little relevance to the investigation. Probabilistic sampling and priorisation can be applied to file carving which will hasten file carving for forensic triage by processing data blocks that are more likely to contain relevant digital traces when investigators are looking for files of a particular kind. The model employs (1) decision theory which is a branch of mathematics that studies decision-making as a choice between several alternative actions and (2) numeric simulation. Decision theoretic analysis allows a file carver to consider the most likely locations of relevant data based on what is known about the distribution of data on the disk. Carving times are reduced by skipping the areas on the disk that are unlikely to contain relevant data. The technique is most useful when applied in a triage situation as the risk of missing relevant evidence is less consequential and is retrievable than when probabilistic sampling is applied in the examination phase [9].

The historical beginnings of the digital forensics field were focused on storage media, especially the user created files on the hard drive. As computer systems develop, probatively valuable forensic evidence is found in a much wider range of locations. For example, the Microsoft operating system stores configuration data in the registry, which is used to run the computer. Analysis of the registry yields very useful forensic evidence in the event of the system being attacked. While the traditional digital forensics tools do not necessarily look at alternative sources of data, efficient tools have been developed to collect evidence from the registry overcome the time-consuming limitations of the preexisting tools. The registry can yield important information (some of it is highly technical, but valuable for the interpretation of other digital evidence) such as the autorun program, recently accessed documents/programs, networks accessed or connected, devices connected, applications installed, login activity, malware activity, running processes and services and timestamp generation [10].

An alternative data reduction method that will reduce storage demands and provide for a more efficient forensic data subset collection process. The method does not replace the need for full analysis, nor is it consistent with the thorough analysis frameworks recommended by authorities such as the Association of Chief Police Officers [11], the European Inion Agency for Network and Information Security [12] and the National Institutes of Justice [13], but it is useful when applied to triage situations and for operational information and intelligence purposes where a quick answer in real time is required. In the data reduction method, the usual forensically sound method of data acquisition is applied. Forensic tools then display and select files of interest that are then preserved in their own container. The size of the preserved data can be substantially smaller than when every bit of data is copied. This data reduction approach can lead to the production of a report that no longer requires a full forensic image of every item seized. Consideration needs to be given to the final purpose of such a report produced as a result of this process. While it is useful to inform operational decision making, caution should be exercised if it is to be used for higher purposes. To be borne in mind is the premise behind the data reduction protocol, that is, it is a process for identifying and selecting inculpatory evidence to the potential exclusion of exculpatory evidence.

The data reduction method can be applied to other situations. For example, in order to compare cases for intelligence purposes or investigations of conspiracy, similar subsets of data from the various cases under investigation can be collected. A full image of the seized item can be made at a later time if necessary when a full forensic analysis is appropriate, for example, when an individual is to be charged or a brief of evidence is required. This approach also has applicability to investigations where digital traces are stored in the cloud. The digital traces of likely probative value can be identified and acquired more rapidly than it would take to download and copy a full image.

The impact of the data reduction approach on organisational storage requirements is significant. In theory, if this approach was applied to the FBI-seized data holdings from 2003 to 2012, the total data held (20 petabytes at that time) could be theoretically reduced to a subset of 4 terabytes. This would result in significant cost savings for storage, and searching the data across cases would also be much faster. An additional benefit is that a reduced subset of the digital traces could be searched while a full forensic image is still being copied. The approach means that a subset image would take 79 s to complete from a 320 GB hard drive, compared with 3 h to complete a full forensic image and another 3 h to verify the copy.

The data reduction principle can be applied in a triage manner. If the subset reveals relevant information on certain items, then the focus of analysis can be on those items. For example, if Internet history and registry files reveal items of interest, then further attention can be given to the full disk image. If nothing of interest is identified, then the item can be set aside for later examination following attention is directed to items that are more likely to provide higher priority evidence [14].

Necessity is the mother of invention

Law enforcement agencies generally managed digital evidence in a similar way and the AFP was no exception. The traditional computer forensics (as it was referred to in the early 2000s) model was a very simple service provider model. An investigator would convey a seized computer to the lab, hand it over to the computer forensics team together with some paperwork with a rudimentary description of the case and then leave with the door closing behind. Some months later the investigator would receive a report describing the results of the examination, perhaps having had the occasional phone call and email along the way. The same model was applied to mobile phones and all manner of devices that started to appear in investigations. As difficult as it was to accept by the digital forensics teams, it was always envisaged that digital evidence examinations would move from the purvey of the specialists, over time, to the investigator. The exponential growth in caseload and data volumes far outpaced the ability of organisations to direct its attention and to respond with appropriate resources in capital, infrastructure, educated and trained examiners and standard operating procedures. The real impetus to move in the direction to inculcate and integrate investigators into the examination process was driven by two specific changes in the field: (1) the extraordinary growth in cases of child exploitation (for a period of time, child exploitation cases comprised half the case load of the AFP Digital Forensics Team) and with the incredible number of images, videos etc. that made up these cases; and (2) the uptake of accessible and desirable mobile phone technology by the community and, therefore, the criminal cohort, where, for example, a single illicit drug importation case would often include around 200 or more mobile phones.

At the time of the dramatic growth in caseload, two high priority crime types became new, major points of focus for the AFP-online child sexual exploitation and terrorism, both domestic and international. These two crime types drove much of the increase in caseload and seized digital traces. In order to meet the challenge of the increased caseload, two major initiatives were implemented to deal with the changes—*GalaxyNet* and *Phone Kiosks*. In themselves, they might seem simple. In concept, they were, and many organisations have implemented similar initiatives. Critically important to the success of the initiatives was the implementation and governance, which I will briefly describe in the succeeding text. Throughout this volume, I speak about the importance of culture to the success of the organisation, and it is no different with these initiatives as the culture of both the team and the broader organisation was critical to their successful implementation and sustainment.

GalaxyNet

The traditional model referenced earlier would involve the digital forensics examiner in all aspects of the analysis, even to the point of classifying images of child exploitation. Clearly, this was an untenable and an unsustainable situation. It was untenable as the examiner has no expertise nor qualifications in the examiner of child abuse material. To draw an analogy, a forensic document examiner will analyse various physical factors of a questioned document, such as handwriting analysis, the ink and the paper, but the examiner will not do any textual analysis of the content of the document.

GalaxyNet was implemented to provide investigators with the forensic product, derived from the digital traces seized in relation to the case, on a system that facilitated interrogation of the evidence in order to identify and flag the files that were relevant to the case. The examiner would then analyse the flagged material to determine the provenance and other technical information of the file. Importantly, the examiner were not required to be in the same location. The AFP, as a national agency, was highly mobile and human capability was often deployed to other locations at short notice. The forensic product could be viewed, interrogated and flagged by the investigator from any AFP office at any time of their choosing. The examiner could then perform analysis from their own location, again at any time of their choosing. The forensic process is broken down as follows (Table 1):

Table 1 Roles of investigator and digital forensics examiner when using GalaxyNet.

Forensic phase	Role	Activity
Identification	Investigator and examiner	In collaboration, identify potential sources of evidence Form a belief or suspicion that the digital evidence is relevant to the terms of the warrant
Preservation	Examiner	Forensic preservation and acquisition of digital evidence Produce a working copy and upload to GalaxyNet Notify the investigator that the evidence is ready for analysis
Analysis	Investigator	Search the working copy on GalaxyNet for information that is relevant to the investigation Flag those items of interest Notify the examiner that investigator analysis is complete
	Examiner	Analyse the flagged items for technical data, e.g. metadata, provenance, location, who accessed and time and date of access Search for exculpatory evidence, mitigating circumstances and data concerning related to potential defences
Reporting	Investigator	Report results of searching and interpretation of the information found Produce brief of evidence, to which the report is attached
	Examiner	Produce independent report regarding the decisions made, actions taken, referencing standard operating procedures and authorisations

Phone kiosks

As mobile phones became widely available to consumers and continued on the innovation pathway so that smartphones became the typical phone received, the forensic service provision model that was in place could not scale to meet the increased demand. Mobile phone forensic tool vendors had begun to develop and make available kiosk type systems, which were fairly simple to use. Although the kiosks are relatively easy to purchase, the risks to the integrity of evidence are significant if they are operated in an uncontrolled way. Several miscarriages of justice have resulted from the misuse of mobile phone kiosks and, conversely, undoubtedly there have been many cases of missed evidence for similar reasons.

To mitigate the risks to the evidence, several controls were put in place.

A market survey and evaluation was conducted to select the most appropriate kiosk.

Before each investigator was permitted to use the kiosk, they were required to undergo a training course conducted by the digital forensic team. The course curriculum included the use of the kiosk, an introduction to digital evidence that included basic information, such as logical versus physical downloads, limitations of the process, knowledge of the potential risks to the evidence and how those risks could be mitigated.

On passing the course the investigator was provided with a certificate which was effectively a licence to drive the kiosk and a unique, secure ID to log on and use the kiosk.

When investigators performed a download of a phone, the report would include their details to which they would attach a copy of their valid and current licence.

The purpose of the download was to provide fast operational information to assist decision making in order to progress investigations, for example, prioritising persons of interest and lines of enquiry. It was not intended to be presented to court but, inevitably, that would happen. The certification or licence plus the standard operating procedures that investigators provided decision makers and courts with a degree of comfort and confidence in the results.

If a phone was problematic or considered to be a high risk, it would be sent to the digital forensics team for initial analysis. Phones were also sent to the digital forensics team for in-depth and confirmatory analysis.

Importantly the kiosks were maintained (updates, cables, supplies, etc.) by the digital forensic team who ensured that the kiosks were operating correctly.

The approach has been and continues to be very successful in alleviating the workload of the digital forensic team by off-loading a significant portion of high volume, low complexity work. The kiosks quickly put important information into the hands of investigators enabling them to make decisions earlier in their investigations. An unintended, yet beneficial consequence of the implementation of both the GalaxyNet and phone kiosk strategies, is that it forced investigators to work with and become comfortable with digital evidence. Digital evidence can be intimidating for investigators, especially when they have had little experience with that type of evidence, yet are aware that the evidence can be inadvertently and easily changed. In addition, by working directly with digital evidence, investigators will also become more familiar with the evidence of their case, rather than taking a passive role when it came to considering digital evidence, enabling better, more informed decision making especially with respect to the state of mind of the individuals (suspect, victim and witnesses) who have some involvement.

Nonphone apps

Database forensics

The database is at the heart of most digital applications and, with the growth in available applications, databases are becoming increasingly important for the storage of important and sensitive information. Database forensics, a subfield of digital forensics, focuses on the detailed analysis of a database including its contents, log files, metadata and data files. The principles of digital forensics apply to database forensics, but the science of the forensic examination of databases is in its relative infancy. A review of the state of database forensics for various relational databases including MySGL, Oracle, SQLite, PostgreSQL, DB2 and SQL Server and NoSQL databases like MongoDB and Redis has been conducted and is a useful resource. The rising popularity of NoSQL databases is due to their ability to handle even larger amounts of data over SQL databases. Several database forensic investigation models, artefacts (including metadata, application schema, triggers, data structure, storage engine and logs), tools for SQLite (including Undark, SQLite Parser, SQLite Doctor, Phoenix Repair and Forensic Browser) and tools for database extraction (including Oxygen Forensic Detective, Xplico, Digital Detective Blade, Kernal Data Recovery, SysTools Analyser, WinHex, NetCat, Windows Forensic Toolchest, SQLCMD and Forensic Toolkit) are reviewed by Chopade and Pachghare [15]. The nuances of database forensics is too technical and broad to discuss in detail in this volume. If database forensics is to become a significant part of your organisation's capability, this is a good place to begin to understand some of the technical implications of the work.

Spotlight

Apple's Spotlight, a preinstalled app on Apple devices, allows a user to search files, mail archives and address books, contacts and other digital assets embedded in a file. Spotlight organises and accesses information using metadata and collects additional data about files such as last opened timestamp, number of times used and dates and times of usage. The Apple operating system (*macOS*) maintains extended attributes in the file system, which Spotlight also collects and indexes. The relevant database can be read and parsed for all of the metadata contained within. By reading the data directly, instead of using macOS utilities, it is possible to recreate the directory structure and ascertain the last time that the record for a particular file or folder was updated. The method was demonstrably useful in the investigation of the theft of intellectual property. The files relevant to the intellect property had been removed from a 500 GB disk at some prior time with no visible remnants present. The disk had a Spotlight index, which indicated that it had been attached to a Mac system, yet the office environment from which the intellectual property was stolen did not have any Mac systems. On examination of the Spotlight metadata, it was found that the complete metadata was present and referenced the files in question. Although the 500 GB source disk had been in heavy use in the office Windows environment, Windows does not interact with Spotlight, so the Spotlight database was preserved despite that heavy use in the approximately 3 month interval between the theft and the investigation [16].

America online instant messaging

While digital forensic practitioners need to maintain proficiency in techniques, they also need to maintain a current understanding of the artefacts that could be recovered from different types of instant messaging products. One such product is America Online Instant Messenger desktop version (AIM). Highlighting the importance of the ongoing development of apps, assumptions based on previous versions are not necessarily correct. Previous versions of AIM would leave digital traces in the cache, but with the upgrade to a Windows 8.1 environment, that no longer held true. Digital traces could, however, be found on the server using corresponding links. Timestamp and file path information can be recovered from the system files (short cuts, event logs, thumb cache and registry keys) of the Windows client application, but artefacts of the contact lists and conversations can only be recovered from the memory dump. Additional data such as portions of conversations and transferred files can potentially be recovered from the swap files and unallocated space. Although most network traffic is encrypted, the IP addresses and URLs may assist in understanding the activity of a suspect [17]. The above three examples give a small indication of the types of specific detail that can be encountered in digital forensics. The understanding of systems and digital traces required of examiners is extensive and is dependant on their foundational education that can then be applied to research in order to acquire the specific knowledge pertaining to each case. Further discussion of some specific apps and the requirements of examiners is discussed in more detail later in this volume.

References

[1] D. Quick, K.-K.R. Choo, Data reduction and data mining framework for digital forensic evidence: storage, intelligence, review and archive, in: Trends and Issues in Crime and Criminal Justice, Australian Institute of Criminology, 2014.

[2] NIST, A Framework for Harmonising Forensic Science Practices and Digital/Multimedia Evidence, National Institutes of Standards and Testing: Organization of Scientific Area Committees for Forensic Science, 2018. Retrieved from, https://www.nist.gov/sites/default/files/documents/2018/01/10/osac_ts_0002.pdf.

[3] E. Casey, D.-O. Jaquet-Chiffelle, Do identities matter? Policing 13 (1) (2017) 21–34.

[4] B. Hitchcock, N. Le-Khac, M. Scanlon, Tiered forensic methodology for digital field triage by non-digital evidence specialists, in: Digital Investigation, DFRWS 2016 Europe – Proceedings of the Third Annual DFRWS Europe, 2016.

[5] R. Lutui, A multidisciplinary digital forensic investigation process model, Bus. Horiz. 59 (6) (2016) 593–604.

[6] B. Cusack, R. Lutui, Updating investigation models for smart phone procedures, in: Proceedings of the 12th Australian Digital Forensics Conference, 2014, pp. 53–63.

[7] C. Stelly, V. Roussev, Nugget: a digital forensics language, in: Digital Investigation: DFRWS 2018 Europe - Proceedings of the Fifth Annual DFRWS Europe, 24, 2018, pp. S38–S47.

[8] A. Asquith, G. Horsman, Let the Robots Do it! Taking a Look at Robotic Process Automation and its Potential Application in Digital Forensics, Forensic Science International: Reports, 2019 (unedited manuscript as accepted for publication).

[9] P. Gladyshev, J. James, Decision-theoretic file carving, Digit. Investig. 22 (2017) 46–61.

[10] D. Patil, B. Meshram, RegForensicTool: evidence collection and analysis of Windows registry, Int. J. Cyber-Sec. Digit. Forensics 5 (2) (2016) 94–105.

[11] Association of Chief Police Officers, ACPO Good Practice Guide for Digital Evidence, http://www.digital-detective.net/acpo-good-practice-guide-for-digital-evidence/, 2012. (Accessed 23 July 2016).

[12] European Union Agency for Network and Information Security, Electronic Evidence – A Basic Guide for First Responders, https://www.enisa.europa.eu/publications/electronic-evidence-a-basic-guide-for-first-responders.

[13] National Institutes of Justice. Electronic Crime Scene Investigation: A Guide for First Responders, second ed. http://www.nij.gov/publications/Pages/publication-detail.aspx?ncjnumber=219941

[14] R. Quick, K.-K.R. Choo, Big Digital Forensic Data, Volume 2: Quick Analysis for Evidence and Intelligence. Springer Briefs on Cyber Security Systems and Networks, Springer, 2018.

[15] R. Chopade, V. Pachghare, Ten years of critical review on database forensics research, Digit. Investig. 29 (2019) 180–197.

[16] Y. Khatri, Investigating spotlight internals to extract metadata, Digit. Investig. 28 (2019) 96–103.

[17] T. Yang, A. Dehghantanha, R. Choo, Z. Muda, Investigating America Online instant messaging application: data remnants on Windows 8.1 client machine, in: Contemporary Digital Forensic Investigations of Cloud and Mobile Applications, 2017, pp. 21–39. (Chapter 3).

Digital forensic organisational capability

6

Digital evidence and digital forensic capabilities have become core investigational capabilities in law enforcement agencies over the past two decades. The importance and need for digital evidence capability has now, however, gone beyond a ubiquitous requirement for law enforcement and regulatory agencies to become a necessary capability in a much wider range of industries and organisations. Any organisation, whether public, private, not-for-profit, or government, has a need to access digital evidence capabilities, whether in-house or through a service provider. I cannot think of an organisation that does not have assets of value, such as intellectual property, personal and private data concerning its employees and the management of funds that is not held, or can be accessed, by a computer system. Digital evidence principles and capabilities are key to not only protecting those valuable assets but also determining if the assets have been subjected to unauthorised access or have been misused.

As oil was to the 20th century and data are to the 21st century, data are now the driver of industry. The growth in and increased complexity of data, its important role as the organisation's intellectual property, the need to retain the privacy of employee and customer data, and the extensive compliance requirements for record keeping have led many organisations to recognise the importance of readiness for digital forensics. Organisational readiness in the management of data is an active process that requires planning and expertise in execution to, for example, respond to security incidents [1].

Most organisations have data retention and disposition policies that provide a schedule for how data should be retained and how they should be disposed. The data retention and disposal policies are subject to the laws and regulations of the jurisdiction in which the organisation is operating. If an organisation is operating in multiple jurisdictions, it is then subject to variability in laws across its organisation from one jurisdiction to the next. In addition, organisations should develop a digital forensic response plan in preparation for when an incident might occur that requires a digital forensic response. The plan should include evidence generators that can capture the evidence of unwanted activities and ensure that they are correctly preserved. Further, a forensic readiness policy details the immediate procedures so that there is a systematic, standardised and legal basis for the admissibility of digital evidence in the event that the evidence is to be presented in legal proceedings, whether they are criminal, civil or administrative proceedings. The policy should enable the gathering of evidence relevant to the investigation without disrupting core business, conducted at a cost that is proportional to the incident and its ramifications, and the evidence has a positive impact of any legal action. Other requirements include financial support for the recruitment and ongoing training of appropriately skilled staff and technological requirements.

Any digital forensic response investigation must comply with the data retention and disposition policies of the jurisdiction and should be consistent with the organisation's

Strategic Leadership in Digital Evidence. https://doi.org/10.1016/B978-0-12-819618-2.00006-1

data and information governance requirements. Other factors to be considered include the impact of litigation holds requirements, releasing and disposing of data in response to court orders, challenges to retention and disposal of data, costs associated with disposition and storage, mitigating and responding to disasters and emergencies and dealing with organisational disciplinary issues.

As digital forensics is related to law and to technology, investigators are expected to do more than just follow the known techniques. The multitude of different crimes that can involve digital evidence, networks and the rapid development of information and communications technology adds to the complexity of any investigation, analysis and interpretation. Further, as legal processes vary from one jurisdiction to the next, organisations need to adopt rigorous and flexible processes in order to meet the specific local requirements. Proper forensic examination not only is restricted to the provenance of law enforcement agencies but also is a responsibility for defence attorneys.

When considering organisational preparedness to mitigate and investigate cyber threats, the needs of incident handling and digital forensics overlap. Maintaining currency of forensic awareness and capability to deal with emerging technology apps is a constant challenge, as is the release of new software and computing formats. As can be seen from the statistics cited earlier, organisations are more likely than not to be subjected to a cyberattack, to the point where it is almost inevitable. Together when fraud and the misuse of organisational resources is taken into account, it is concerning that, generally speaking, the vast majority of organisations have little awareness of forensic readiness and are grossly underprepared to respond to an investigation that requires the production of artefacts concerning any incident to which they have been subjected [2]. The lack of appropriate forensic readiness will potentially compromise any legal recourse and rectification.

With the understanding that digital forensic techniques and processes are now being referenced for other purposes, the competition for skills and knowledge that are infinite supply will become even keener than it has been. An additional purpose for digital evidence skills is in the archiving and disposition of records and maintaining collections of historical records for which government agencies and other organisations in compliance with laws and regulations governing the management of records. There are some factors that lead to the desirability for digital evidence principles to be applied to other purposes, including the growing rates at which emails are sent across the world, and the repurposing of email from a means of communication to now also being used for task management and personal archiving. Collecting institutions, currently managing their collections by manual processes, need to improve their methods of discovery, identification and redaction, or they will lose the trust of donors and accumulate a backlog of unprocessed material. This is particularly fraught when the managed information contains personal and personally identifying information. Further, employing digital forensic methods in archives can assist archivists in discovering valuable information for clients, such as credit card numbers, phone numbers, email addresses, social security numbers and other private information. By employing digital forensic methods, light has been shed on the misuse of organisational resources, including illegal and politically sensitive records, such as pornography and misogynistic content. Digital forensic processes assist organisations in gaining an understanding of, for example, its equal employment opportunity culture by identifying toxic language that might be used in communications between employees [3].

References

[1] N.M. Karie, S.M. Karume, Digital forensic readiness in organisations: issues and challenges, J. Digit. Forensic Secur. Law 12 (4) (2017) 43–53.

[2] N. Ab Rahman, G. Kessler, R. Choo, Implications of emerging technologies to incident handling and digital forensic strategies: a routine activity theory, in: Contemporary Digital Forensic Investigations of Cloud and Mobile Applications, Elsevier, 2017, pp. 131–146.

[3] W. Vinh-Doyle, Appraising email (using digital forensics): techniques and challenges, Arch. Manuscripts 45 (1) (2017) 18–30.

Education and training

7

Apart from the true leadership that one brings to building, leading and managing a digital evidence capability, in addition to quality assurance, there is no more important facet than education and training that to your team. Although this might seem to be obvious for any professional endeavour, it is especially true in digital evidence. It is not possible to prescribe every scenario in every case that your team will encounter, but if the individuals have sound fundamental and applied knowledge, plus a willingness to continue to learn, they will be able to meet the needs of each case they encounter through the application of good decision-making.

There are a number of documents that have been produced by experienced professionals in the field and the subdisciplines of digital evidence, which provide good guidance on the education that digital forensic examiners should have before entering the field, and subsequent ongoing training that they should undertake. For example, the task group that developed the framework for harmonising forensic science practices and digital/multimedia evidence describes the foundational sciences for the various subdisciplines including not only biology, physics and mathematics but also computer science, computer engineering, image science, video and television engineering, acoustics, linguistics, anthropology, statistics and data science [1].

I do have one difference of opinion with the current convention for digital forensic examiners though. It is a requirement for digital evidence courses to include some general chemistry and/or biology in their degree course if the institution is seeking accreditation through the Forensic Science Education Programs Accreditation Commission of the American Academy of Forensic Science [2]. In my experience, this is a waste of time and an unnecessary cost to students for which they will receive little return. Many students select digital evidence as that is what they are interested in, and there is little crossover benefit to be gained from studying the other subjects. Given the rapid evolution and development of new technologies in the consumer and business markets, I would be more interested in seeing students spending more time in learning those technologies or other more relevant subjects such as developing a stronger knowledge of law.

As alluded to earlier, the role of the digital forensic practitioner requires several cross-disciplinary facets including an understanding of practice, procedure, technology and law, underpinned by ethics. Due to the current and predicted shortage of suitable candidates for information security jobs, the training in cyber forensics has been the subject of much attention by the governments of several countries, including the United States (NSA—National Security Agency Center of Academic Excellence in Cyber Defence Education) and the United Kingdom (GCHQ—Government Communications Headquarters National Cyber Security Centre). These initiatives are supported by additional work from organisations such as the United States National Institute of Standards and Technology Cybersecurity Workforce Framework to ensure the consistent use of terminology [3].

Strategic Leadership in Digital Evidence. https://doi.org/10.1016/B978-0-12-819618-2.00007-3

To assist in digital forensic training and exercise, several data sets are available for training purposes including (1) the National Institute of Standards and Technology library of Computer Forensics Reference Data Sets that cover a range of scenarios including hacking, data leakage, registry forensics, drone images, Russian tea room, memory images and mobile device images [4], and (2) Digital Corpora that cover cell phone dumps, disk images, files, network packet dumps and scenarios [5].

Despite the substantial teaching resources outlined above, the generation of real digital evidence is by suspects. Some researchers in digital evidence have been able to encourage senior students to enrich their learning by generating a trail of evidence, which provided them with a greater awareness of how evidence is formed, file provenance and root cause analysis. Senior students, who are generating the evidence, were buddying junior students, so they needed to develop a good understanding of best practice and procedures in the discipline. The researchers enhanced the learning experience by partnering the students from schools in two different countries (Norway and the United States) where creating and analysing digital forensic data.

The American Academy of Forensic Sciences, Forensic Science Education Programs Accreditation Commission revised its accreditation standards for 2018 (FEPAC, 2017) and 2019 (FEPAC, 2019). The 2019 version is amended to include a 'survey of forensic science' as a general curriculum requirement, and the option to include business statistics within the mathematics component. The 2019 undergraduate program standard still retains a requirement to complete studies in physics, chemistry and biology but has removed the requirement for a minimum of six semester hours '...that provide breadth in traditional forensic sciences (e.g. DNA, latent prints, trace chemistry, microscopy, crime scene reconstructions, etc...'. For the postgraduate courses, the 2019 standard has removed the requirement for studies in forensic biology but still retains pattern evidence. Additional clarity is provided for the requirements of the research project.

I do have one difference of opinion with the current convention for digital forensics examiners though. It is a requirement for digital evidence courses to include some general chemistry and/or biology in their degree course if the institution is seeking accreditation through the Forensic Science Education Programs Accreditation Commission of the American Academy of Forensic Science [2]. In my experience, this is a waste of time and an unnecessary cost to students for which they will receive little return. Many students select digital evidence as that is what they are interested in, and there is little crossover benefit to be gained from studying the other subjects. Given the rapid evolution and development of new technologies in the consumer and business markets, I would be more interested in seeing students spending more time in learning the underpinning science of emerging those technologies or other more relevant subjects such as developing a stronger knowledge of law.

The practice of digital evidence would benefit greatly from taking a knowledge management approach to education and training. Knowledge management is the process of capturing, storing, retrieving, managing and representing knowledge. Knowledge management provides a competitive business advantage. There exists a range of knowledge management techniques that are applicable to the field but are dependent on the ethos of the organisation. It is particularly useful as many of the traditional digital evidence tools are becoming less effective, and new tools and techniques are required [6]. I have found knowledge management to be exceptionally useful where it has been applied and especially so in digital evidence as new knowledge is developing rapidly in parallel with developments in technology. As described elsewhere the breakneck speed at which technology changes constantly presents new challenges, often requiring the examiner to solve problems that are unique to each specific case. Under the circumstances in which most digital forensic capabilities operate with time pressures and case backlogs, that knowledge would be locked away when the file is closed and not available to the wider team. A knowledge management strategy will capture each specific problem(s) encountered and the solution that the examiner was able to design and implement to address the problem. When indexed and shared, the ever growing repository was very useful to the team, especially as the team was geographically dispersed.

References

[1] NIST, A Framework for Harmonizing Forensic Science Practices and Digital/Multimedia Evidence, National Institutes of Standards and Testing: Organization of Scientific Area Committees for Forensic Science, 2018. Retrieved from https://www.nist.gov/sites/default/files/documents/2018/01/10/osac_ts_0002.pdf.

[2] Forensic Science Education Programs Accreditation Commission, Accreditation Standards, 2020, Retrieved from https://www.fepac-edu.org/sites/default/files/FEPAC%20Standards%2002152020.pdf.

[3] L. Carthy, E. Ovensen, R. Little, I. Sutherland, H. Read, Committing the Perfect Crime: A Teaching Perspective, European Conference on Cyber Warfare and Security, 2018.

[4] NIST, Computer Forensic Reference Data Sets, The National Institute of Standards and Technology, 2019. Retrieved from https://www.cfreds.nist.gov.

[5] Digital Corpora, Retrieved from, 2019. https://digitalcorpora.org.

[6] R. Verma, P. Bansal, Scope and managing knowledge in digital forensics, in: Proceedings of the International Conference on Sustainable Computing in Science, Technology and Management (SUSCOM-2019), 2019. Retrieved from https://papers.ssrn.com/sol3/papers.cfm?abstract_id=3363040.

Quality assurance

8

Digital evidence concerns the evidence, or digital traces, produced as a result of digital technologies, most commonly computer processing and involves range of devices. Technology is related to engineering with a basis in science and mathematics. Technology involves the manipulation of matter and the application of defined things, such as devices, systems, methods and procedures to perform a practical function [1]. As digital evidence is applied to legal processes, it then follows that it should be subject to the same admissibility requirements as other scientific evidence.

However, technology is a socially shaped phenomenon meaning that design and function are the result of social processes rather than of scientific-technological rationality. The extension of this theory leads to the understanding that technological development does not follow a fixed and predictable, linear pathway. It is subject to contested ideas, controversies and differences of opinion between various social groups. One such example is the modern day Internet itself, which was not conceived and designed with security at the forefront of its design principles, but as a means of communication between like-minded people. The Internet is, therefore, subject to inherent security vulnerabilities. Had the first Internet design principles included native security, such as would have been expected if it designed in a framework of scientific-technological rationality, as a priority rather than the result of social processes, it is highly doubtful that it would have been taken up by the world's population to the extent that it has nor would it be as successful as it is.

As a consequence, socially driven digital technology leads to a very complex environment in which the digital evidence examiner is endeavouring to make sense of seemingly disparate forms of data, in a consistent and reliable manner. To ensure the reliability of results, some form of quality assurance framework is pertinent. Quality assurance in digital evidence, however, continues to be a vexed issue with many opposing views expressed by different parties. There are many reasons for this, and I encountered most of them when I first entered the field in 2002 and continue to encounter them to this day. Let me say from the outset, the guiding principle is that digital evidence is primarily concerned with evidence that will potentially impact on the human rights of an individual, whether they are an alleged perpetrator or victim of crime, or impact on the viability of an organisation, or impact on myriad other situations to which digital evidence is applied. There is no room for error as it is critical that the result of digital evidence analysis is correct, whether that be for testimony in a criminal trial or the remediation of a cyberattack on a network computer system, or to be used for intelligence purposes in conflict situations between states and nonstate actors.

Within days of my commencement in this field, I met with my new counterparts as managers of the digital evidence capabilities for their respective state and federal

Strategic Leadership in Digital Evidence. https://doi.org/10.1016/B978-0-12-819618-2.00008-5

agencies throughout Australia. The subject of accreditation arose for discussion. Almost without exception, my counterparts described accreditation in negative terms with the almost consensus view that accreditation was evil and was something to be resisted. It was understood that their expressed collective view was representative of the majority view of participants in the field around the world. After listening to their views, I asked the question '[a]s I understand it, you download tools from the internet, or share tools between each other, or obtain commercial tools from vendors. What have you done to confirm that the tools you use perform in the way that they are purported to perform, have performed without error, and that the evidence you use to prosecute individuals is reliable? Can your reports be trusted? Accreditation is not having some random person look over your shoulder and criticise your work, but your peers, the other people sitting around this table, to verify the work that you have undertaken to an acceptable standard'. I also advised that, at the Australian Federal Police, accreditation to ISO 17025, the standard that is primarily used for accreditation in forensic science, will be implemented for digital evidence as it has been implemented for the other forensic disciplines. Almost to a person, heads around the table went down as people looked at their hands.

The Australian Federal Police followed through on this promise and became the first digital evidence laboratory in the world to become accredited to ISO 17025. It has served the AFP very well as it meets several objectives including the provision of a (1) minimum acceptable standard leading to the production of fair and reliable testimony in which courts can confidently believe that work has been conducted by a competent person in an approved facility and that the work has been peer reviewed; (2) guiding framework for decision-making and appropriate management oversight; (3) risk mitigation strategy that protects the integrity of the organisation through the preemptive identification of potential errors; and (4) framework for continuous improvement, a necessity for a rapidly evolving discipline where the substrate continues to change in form.

Although often debated, it is now generally accepted that the data comprising digital evidence are not 'fact' but are in fact uncertain and can contain errors. The errors can result from system faults or be introduced by human intervention. The potential system faults can result from faulty software, e.g. bugs, or hardware of the target devices. Those introduced by human error can include faulty digital evidence tools or the incorrect use of the tools such as incorrect application or use outside the tool's recommended scope.

Quality assurance and accreditation issues in digital evidence have been prominent in the literature in recent years, especially in the United Kingdom and primarily due to the appropriate scrutiny under which digital evidence has been placed. The United Kingdom Forensic Science Regulator has expressed the priority intent to work with all National Police Chiefs' Council relevant portfolios to ensure their compliance with requirements and appropriate quality standards [2]. Importantly the regulator highlighted the importance for the police to no longer procure digital forensic services from organisations that are not yet compliant with accreditation standards. These statements represent very important policy positions to ensure that courts can be confident and comfortable that they are being provided with an accurate reflection of the evidence and testimony that justly interprets that evidence.

In addition to that policy position, the regulator is overseeing the development of several standards for digital evidence, including:

- Cell site analysis and communications data, but the regulator has noted that there is a lack of scientific scrutiny in this specialist area with limited published, peer-reviewed research. It was further noted that specific areas being addressed include the difference between technical interpretation and opinion evidence in cell site analysis, the assessment of uncertainty in call data records, the assessment of uncertainties of methods used within cell site analysis and the interpretation models for providing opinion in cell site analysis.
- Network forensics, which covers the screening and extraction of data from a business's networked computer system.
- Open-source intelligence (Internet intelligence and investigations), which includes core Internet use, overt Internet intelligence and investigations, and authorised covert Internet intelligence and investigations.

The progress by UK policing organisations in meeting compliance requirements slowed in 2018 due to competing resource pressures. It was also noted that commercial viability needs to be considered when procuring services from accredited providers as the incentive to purchase services for the lowest price, as governments are generally seeking to do in the principle of 'value for money'. By November 2017, within law enforcement, 12 legal entities (of a total of 46) were accredited for imaging storage devices, three for data extraction, six for mobile phones and two CCTV. Only four of 20–30 commercial providers to the criminal justice system in the United Kingdom had gained accreditation, and smaller providers had made no progress [3]. This has led to expressed concerns by smaller providers of insufficient incentive to pursue accreditation as policing continues to award contracts to nonaccredited providers, and the '… [perceived] lack of commitment to quality standards in policing'. Quality concerns were a motivation for a review of the provision of forensic services in the United Kingdom [4], which resulted in an implementation plan that included building capacity into the system so that all providers of digital forensic services can be accredited [5]. Quality costs money. As stated above, accreditation to ISO 17025 represents the minimum acceptable standard when digital evidence is used in legal proceedings. Purchasers must ask themselves whether they can afford not to purchase a quality service.

The issue of accreditation continues to remain somewhat contentious. While most jurisdictions support accreditation in some form, usually to ISO 17025, or at least to ISO 17020, for almost all of the forensic sciences, some resistance remains for the accreditation of digital evidence providers. Although there is broad support for accreditation of digital evidence to ISO 17025, some practitioners and organisations support the application of other standards such as ISO 27037, 27,041, 27,042, 27,044 and 27,050, albeit in the acknowledgement that the standards other than ISO 17025 and ISO 17020 are actually guidelines rather than expected minimum standards of practice [6]. There continues to be substantial commentary on this subject with much of it ill informed and therefore not reflected here. The strength of ISO 17025 lies not only in the technical aspects of the standard but also in the requirements for the accredited organisation to demonstrate management competence, validation of the tools employed, competence of staff, ability to anticipate, detect and remediate errors, verification of results etc. that is subject to peer review and independent, external review. The minimum requirements as enunciated through ISO 17025, if not met, will present substantial risk to the quality, and, therefore, the efficacy of digital evidence practice and subsequent results that might lead to, as it has in the past led to the tragedy of miscarriages of justice and to the failure to apprehend a criminal who is free to continue to offend [7].

It is useful to compare the quality assurance processes between the forensic disciplines of DNA, latent fingerprints and digital evidence, and to reflect on the historic scrutiny to which each discipline has been subjected. As a relative new forensic discipline and unlike the other more traditional disciplines with longer histories, digital evidence has remained relatively unchallenged from high profile reviews of its capacity to provide reliable evidence. The lack of challenge is despite the fact that digital evidence often has been the subject of criticism for the failure to promptly and comprehensively disclose evidence. It is important to note that '…as soon as human interaction is introduced into a process, there is the possibility of human-related error … therefore actions to prevent human error should occur'. Multiple recent studies published in the academic literature have drawn the common observation that there are few formalised and enforceable peer-reviewed and quality assurance procedures enforced in digital evidence. Moreover, the implementation of a quality management system is dependent on the availability of budget, as though it is a discretionary budget item, or that it is a box to be checked to successfully tender for work for compliance purposes rather than being regarded as a fundamental part of a digital evidence capability. The central premise for implementing a quality assurance framework is to improve and maintaining high-quality work that provides confidence and assurance to stakeholders and customers.

There are five hierarchical levels of peer review that can be undertaken in digital evidence as a part of a structured quality assurance process. In descending order of resource intensity, they are:

- blind reexamination of the entire case,
- verification review of the examiner's findings,
- conceptual peer review that ensures the correct interpretation of the work but makes assumptions that certain steps were completed correctly,
- sense review that checks that the case file makes sense but involves no checking of evidence,
- proof check which is no more than a light administrative review [8].

Due to budget and time constraints, the most effective forms of review, blind reexamination and verification review are unlikely to be conducted except in exceptional circumstances. Further, in smaller organisations and due to the complexity and wide variety of types of digital evidence (devices, operating systems, applications etc.), it is unlikely that a sufficient number of expert staff will be available who can adequately review the work in any meaningful way that fulfills blind examination review and verification review. However, insufficient numbers of staff cannot be an excuse for noncompliance with what are considered to be the minimum acceptable standards of conduct in digital evidence as defined by accreditation. In effect, such an approach concedes that the accepted quality of evidence is determined by the provider and not the customer and stakeholders as represented by the judicial forum in which the results are to be presented and weighed. It is essential to be born in mind that the evidence is being used to determine the guilt or innocence of a person accused of committing a crime, and justice for a victim and has major consequences when presented in court. An alternative school of thought suggests that fact checking and verification should be viewed as a job for the defence [9]. Such a suggestion contradicts a prosecutor's and the digital evidence examiner's professional responsibilities. No matter which jurisdiction a case is being tried, prosecutors carry the responsibility of ensuring that a defendant '…is accorded procedural justice, that guilt is decided upon the basis if sufficient evidence, and that special precautions are taken to prevent and to rectify the conviction of innocent persons'. [10] All parties to an investigation and subsequent prosecution have a professional and ethical responsibility to ensure that all reasonable steps have been taken to ensure the validity of the presented evidence.

Some alternative processes that meet the requirements of accreditation and, therefore, attain better practice and meet the intent of the accreditation standards could be employed. Such processes include using dual investigators as an extension of dual tooling[a] whereby examiners divide a given case and collaborate in the examination, thus providing a culture of ongoing peer review, and the random sampling of cases for intensive review [8] (Fig. 8.1).

There exist various possible approaches to assuring the quality of digital forensics for court noting that any scheme chosen needs to be viable in implementation and value for money. The approaches can be categorised into three groups: (1) individual

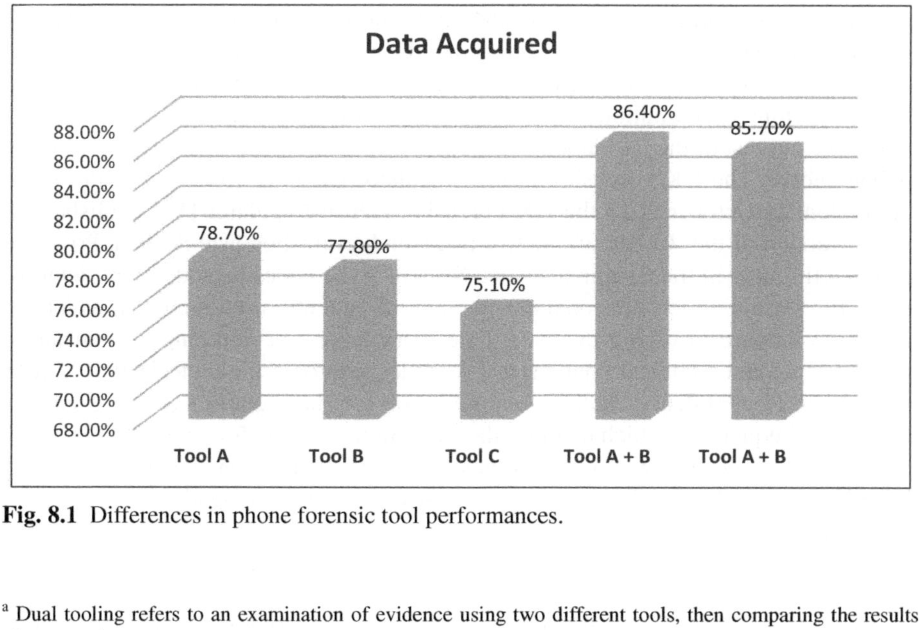

Fig. 8.1 Differences in phone forensic tool performances.

[a] Dual tooling refers to an examination of evidence using two different tools, then comparing the results between the two.

accreditation, (2) laboratory accreditation and (3) court procedures. An additional risk is caused by the presence of multiple, rival accrediting organisations that will confuse the central issue of quality assurance as the rival organisations will tend to favour one system, their preferred system in which they have invested, over another rival system. Proponents of alternative systems, such as certification using 'standards', will argue that ISO 17025, which is regarded as the mainstay of accreditation in forensic science in adversarial justice jurisdictions and, therefore, digital forensics, is not the framework that is best suited for the assurance of digital forensics. Such an argument is based on certain characteristics where digital forensics differs from other evidence types, including, but not limited to, the fast pace of development in digital devices, operating systems and applications; one-off processes that might be used for unique cases; the cost of compliance with accreditation requirements and the lack of a 'laboratory setting' for the conduct of digital forensic examinations [11]. I strongly refute this assertion as most, if not all, of the so-called alternative frameworks are unsuitable for digital forensics in a legal setting. Firstly, they are not standards at all, but are guidelines and therefore do not undergo external and independent scrutiny for compliance. Secondly and perhaps the most critically important, they do not include any review and assessment of expert testimony that has been presented in court, a critical feature of accreditation. Such review and assessment are sought from both prosecution and defence counsel, and from the examiner's supervisor. Despite noting the differences in opinion concerning quality assurance, tool testing and validation, most leading authors support accreditation to ISO 17025 for digital evidence and its place as, effectively, a mandatory requirement in the practice of digital forensics. The fundamental tenet of ISO 17025 is as a standard to 'ensure organisational competence and maintain public confidence that standards in digital forensics are maintained' [12]. It is incumbent on organisations to demonstrate the reliability of the methods they use.

Although it is a topic of discussion in many jurisdictions, much of the public debate concerning accreditation in digital evidence has occurred in the United Kingdom where the interest of the Parliament has been drawn numerous times in addition to the public debate. The UK Forensic Science Regulator has been front and centre in the discussion. In October 2017 the UK Forensic Science Regulator [13] published the fourth version of the 'Codes of Practice and Conduct for Forensic Science Providers and Practitioners in the Criminal Justice System'. The codes provide more detail on standards pertaining to occasional experts and infrequently used methods, which occasionally feature in digital evidence case work when encountering an unusual or recently emerged technical challenge. The codes reinforce the concept that '...[the] same level of confidence shall be required whether the method is to be used routinely or infrequently', which includes the validation of methods and the demonstrated competence of the staff who perform those methods. In addition, experts who testify infrequently or who are from overseas are to fulfil certain obligations and admissibility requirements including to be bound by the code of conduct. Notably for digital evidence, the codes set a schedule by which organisations are expected to meet accreditation requirements [13].

As we have already seen, the digital evidence examination process, as it involves human input to the process, is therefore subject to human error. The Task Group that developed *A Framework for Harmonising Forensic Science Practices and Digital/ Multimedia Evidence* in the United States notes the importance of the consideration of error mitigation in digital/multimedia evidence [14, 15]. Importantly, the task group notes that even when examination techniques are working perfectly, there remains the potential for cognitive bias, observer error and other nontechnical sources of error, some of which are discussed in other sections of this volume. A lack of examiner competence can lead to overlooked and misinterpreted digital traces, and an organisational management that prioritises speed over quality can severely impact the reliability of examinations.

Although a significant proportion of those persons who examine and interpret digital evidence still regard 'digital evidence' as a fact-based discipline, there are many sources of potential error for which mitigation, detection and correction policies and actions need to be in place. Some examples are provided in other sections of this text, for example, potential errors in the clock function of devices. One source of potential error can be due to the impact of supply voltages, temperature, radiation or aging of the transistors to the memory cells of processors.

As it currently stands, each organisation operating under an ISO 17025 accreditation framework is able to determine its quality assurance processes. There exists a lack of formalised quality assurance procedures, such as verification or peer review, within digital forensics. Although peer review is mentioned by the Scientific Working Group on Digital Evidence, no description as to how this should be undertaken is provided [16, 17]. Effectively, this leaves organisations the room to determine its own verification and peer review procedures, providing that they meet the requirements of the accreditation. Importantly, as addressed elsewhere in this volume, despite the now discredited traditional view that digital evidence is fact based, digital evidence is subject to error. Therefore, to ensure the elimination of bias, it is critical that verification and peer review processes are conducted independently.

As mentioned earlier, I have had the opportunity to work within and observe many organisations that provide forensic science services. From this experience, I would estimate that around 90% of forensic science providers have a poor implementation of their quality framework. Without dwelling on the shortcomings, I can offer the following recommendations based on observation and experience across a number of organisations. Most importantly, a one-size-fits-all quality manual does not exist, reflected by many organisations that have tried to copy the manual from one organisation that, at a superficial level, appears to be similar and to provide similar services and transplant it to their own organisation—simply, it never works. A quality manual is a reflection of the forensic science provider in the context in which they operate, including its place within a larger organisation and the system in which it operates. A quality manual should follow the principle of 'do what you say, and say what you do'.

Accreditation to ISO 17025 (general requirements for the competence of testing and calibration laboratories) for forensic science can be seen as an overwhelming undertaking. It introduces new terminology and concepts that can be discomforting. It can also be confusing to distinguish between technical and management responsibilities and how they might intersect. As a first step, it is recommended that the organisation undertakes a management system certification to ISO 9001, but, obviously, taking exception to the clauses that deal with the design of products and/or services. ISO 17025 is derived from, and based on, the ISO 9001 framework; therefore, once completed, the hard work is done.

To implement ISO 9001 certification, engaged leadership from the most senior person through to all levels of supervision and staff is most effective. A common mistake is to leave the process to the 'quality person'. Engaged leadership that seeks and encourages input from all levels will inculcate the organisation with a quality culture and gain a strong commitment from most, if not all, of the people within the organisation. A strong quality culture will encourage a quality-first approach without the sense that people are 'being watched', and people will then voluntarily identify risks before they become issues.

Once the ISO 9001 is implemented,[b] the ISO 17025 accreditation can be pursued. Many organisations make the mistake of giving the responsibility for the accreditation process to the 'quality team' or the 'quality person'. It has been incredible to see how often the misfit within the organisation has been designated as the quality person or the task of accreditation has been assigned as a 'development opportunity'. The quality manager should have exceptional people skills and have a somewhat sceptical view of the quality process. If this seems confounding, there is a reason. As was mentioned earlier, 90% of forensic quality systems are poorly implemented and reflect the conventional or established approach to quality. They are typically overly bureaucratic and involve volumes of documentation. Moreover, poorly implemented quality systems usually require the professional scientists, who have been educated, trained and employed at great expense, to be performing many duties of paperwork, checking and rechecking. Some organisations will have work checked three, four and five times, where errors are still identified late in the checking processes. My view is that this occurs for two main reasons: (1) earlier checkers in the process, who have their own work to perform, rush through the checking process in the belief that a later checker will note any errors, and (2) sheer and absolute boredom, as they spending more time checking other people's work than in doing their own scientific and case work.

Finally, when writing the quality manual, ensure that it is not overly prescriptive, which is a commonly made mistake. Digital evidence, more than any other forensic discipline, evolves and changes rapidly, and the details of the changes cannot feasibly be captured in documentation. Instead the quality manual should comprise a series of considerations with decisions that the examiner will make based on the training that they have undertaken.[c] The digital evidence quality manual for the Australian Federal Police, with which ISO 17025 accreditation was attained, comprised a total of

[b] ISO 9001 certification is not necessary if it is intended that ISO 17025 forensic accreditation is to be pursued. But the ISO 9001 certification reflects a record of achievement of the milestone and the hard work that your people have put in. Moreover, it was valued by the people and engendered a sense of pride in the workplace.

[c] Training for digital evidence examiners should be regular and of high quality. Training should not only comprise the use of tools which, although important, is not the most important, but should proportionately be spent on fundamental understanding of devices and systems as they develop.

26 pages. This was after two previous attempts (drafted, but not submitted) that were approximately 500 and 600 pages, respectively. The 26 page manual met the requirements of accreditation and served the organisation well.

References

[1] P. Brey, Theorizing technology and its role in crime and law enforcement, in: M. McGuire, T. Holt (Eds.), The Routloudge Handbook of Technology, Crime and Justice, Taylor & Francis Group, 2017.

[2] United Kingdom Forensic Science Regulator, Annual Report 17 November 2017 to 16 November 2018, 2019, Retrieved from https://assets.publishing.service.gov.uk/government/uploads/system/uploads/attachment_data/file/786137/FSRAnnual_Report_2018_v1.0.pdf?_ga=2.127790285.1384007655.1566857069-1676743936.1458493850.

[3] United Kingdom Forensic Science Regulator, Annual Report: November 2016–November 2017, 2018, Retrieved from https://assets.publishing.service.gov.uk/government/uploads/system/uploads/attachment_data/file/786137/FSRAnnual_Report_2018_v1.0.pdf.

[4] Home Office, APCC, NPCC, Forensics Review: Review of the Provision of Forensic Science to the Criminal Justice System in England and Wales, 2018, Retrieved from https://assets.publishing.service.gov.uk/government/uploads/system/uploads/attachment_data/file/800447/Joint-review-of-forensics-provision-July-2018.pdf.

[5] Retrieved from. https://assets.publishing.service.gov.uk/government/uploads/system/uploads/attachment_data/file/796812/Forensics-implementation-plan-April-2019.pd.

[6] House of Lords, Forensic Science and the Criminal Justice System: A Blueprint for Change, House of Lords: Science and Technology Select Committee, May 1, 2019. Retrieved from https://publications.parliament.uk/pa/ld201719/ldselect/ldsctech/333/33302.htm.

[7] E. Casey, The checquered past and risky future of digital forensics, Aust. J. Forensic Sci. 51 (5) (2019) 1–16.

[8] H. Page, G. Horseman, A. Saran, J. Foster, A review of quality procedures in the UK forensic sciences: what can the field of digital forensics learn? Sci. Justice 59 (1) (2018) 83–92.

[9] O. Bowcott, Police Mishandling Digital Evidence, Experts Warn, 15 May 2018, Retrieved from https://www.theguardian.com/law/2018/may/15/police-mishandling-digital-evidence-forensic-experts-warn.

[10] American Bar Association, Rule 3.8: Special Responsibilities of a Prosecutor - Comment, 2020, Retrieved from https://www.americanbar.org/groups/professional_responsibility/publications/model_rules_of_professional_conduct/rule_3_8_special_responsibilities_of_a_prosecutor/comment_on_rule_3_8/.

[11] P. Sommer, Accrediting digital forensics: what are the choices? Digit. Investig. 25 (2018) 116–120.

[12] G. Horsman, Tool testing and reliability issues in the field of digital forensics, Digit. Investig. 28 (2019) 163–175.

[13] United Kingdom Forensic Science Regulator, Codes of practice and conduct for forensic science providers and practitioners in the criminal justice system, 2017, Issue 4. Retrieved from https://assets.publishing.service.gov.uk/government/uploads/system/uploads/attachment_data/file/651966/100_-_2017_10_09_-_The_Codes_of_Practice_and_Conduct_-_Issue_4_final_web_web_pdf__2_.pdf.

[14] NIST, A Framework for Harmonizing Forensic Science Practices and Digital/Multimedia Evidence, National Institutes of Standards and Testing: Organization of Scientific Area Committees for Forensic Science, 2018. Retrieved from https://www.nist.gov/sites/default/files/documents/2018/01/10/osac_ts_0002.pdf.

[15] SWGDE, Establishing Confidence in Digital Forensic Results by Error Mitigation Analysis. Scientific Working Group on Digital Evidence, version 1.7, 2017, Retrieved from https://www.swgde.org/documents/Current%20Documents/SWGDE%20Establishing%20Confidence%20in%20Digital%20Forensic%20Results%20by%20Error%20Mitigation%20Analysis.

[16] N. Sunde, I. Dror, Cognitive and human factors in digital forensics: problems, challenges, and the way forward, Digit. Investig. 29 (2019) 101–108.

[17] SWGDE, Establishing confidence in digital forensic results by error mitigation analysis. Version 2.0, 2018 (November 20, 2018).

Human factors

9

From the beginning of digital evidence's formation as a discipline, it has been generally considered to be fact-based evidence. Although anecdotal, conversations with stakeholders within the justice system, including members of the judiciary, revealed a continued widespread belief that digital evidence is still considered to be fact-based as that is the way that it has been presented in court and has remained unchallenged by defence counsel. While the assertion that digital evidence is fact based has always been erroneous and without foundation, that assertion could now quite rightly be considered to be a fallacy. Research on miscarriages of justice in multiple jurisdictions has highlighted the prevalent issue of human error in forensic science, with a particular focus on cognitive bias in several forensic disciplines. In recent years, digital forensics has increasingly taken a more scientific approach to analysis and interpretation of evidence accompanied by an increased focus on quality management, error mitigation, tool testing and verification methodologies. A growing number of peak organisations and professional bodies recognise digital evidence as a discipline of forensic science and, therefore, are subject to uncertainties, vulnerabilities, limitations and the potential for error in a similar way to other forensic disciplines.

Whereas in its infancy as the discipline of digital evidence the tools and technology were perceived to be the main instruments in the digital forensic process, that perception has now moved to one of a better understanding the role of the human in the practice of the discipline. The shift in understanding that humans are central to the discipline of digital evidence and recognising that humans are subject to human factors and human error, it follows that cognitive factors and their impact on decision-making must also be taken into consideration when analysing and interpreting digital evidence. The core processes of digital forensics are increasingly understood to be aligned to those of other forensic disciplines; therefore the other disciplines are an appropriate starting point for the consideration of the influence of human factors and the mitigation of any resultant affects. The potential for human error that has led to miscarriages of justice or overturned convictions has been well established in other forensic science disciplines and has now been found to impact digital evidence, specifically the analysis and interpretation of evidence concerning CCTV recordings, SIM cards, DVD content and web content [1].

There exists a well-established taxonomy comprising sources of cognitive biases that may affect forensic decisions within the digital forensic process. The cognitive biases arise from the way in which the brain processes information. Biases are neither intentional nor conscious, but are related to emotions such as confidence, frustration, sorrow, anger, personal responsibility and concern about future consequences [2, 3]. Much of the work of digital forensic practitioners is likely to include child sexual exploitation investigations in which the forensic practitioner may be required to view graphic images, video and online communication which can serve to greatly impact the emotional state of the practitioner. The taxonomy comprising seven levels has

Strategic Leadership in Digital Evidence. https://doi.org/10.1016/B978-0-12-819618-2.00009-7

been applied to other forensic disciplines to mitigate the impact of bias. The same taxonomy can also be applied to digital evidence: (1) the cognitive architecture and the brain, (2) training and motivation, (3) organisational factors, (4) base rate expectations, (5) irrelevant case information, (6) reference materials and (7) case evidence.

One of the major factors that can contribute to bias and pose a risk to objectivity is the traditional integration of digital forensic teams into the investigational teams. I describe it as traditional as the first digital forensic teams were a specialised function within investigational teams, such as fraud squads. Some law enforcement agencies persist with this model to this day which presents a significant risk to the integrity of the analysis and interpretation of the evidence. It should be noted that the risk does not impugn the integrity of the officers and examiners involved, but the risk posed by a close functional and administrative arrangement is difficult to disentangle and is unfair to the people who are working in close proximity. I strongly recommend that the digital forensic capability is maintained administratively independent from the investigational teams. From time to time, I would experience pressure to permanently second a digital forensic team member to an investigational team, and occasionally, investigators would lobby to have their own digital forensic team. Such a permanent arrangement was not in anyone's long-term interests and I always resisted it. To meet investigators' needs, however, an outreach program was developed that would include the opportunity for digital forensics team members to second for 1–2 days per week with investigations teams, or to second a member to a task force on a short-term basis. By maintaining the separation,

1. the organisation could appropriately and flexibly allocate finite resources to geographical and functional areas of highest need;
2. consistency and quality assurance of digital forensic processes, procedures and training could be maintained;
3. digital forensic practitioners would undertake a wider range of work to assist their continued development, and, more importantly, they would not encounter a disproportionate amount of noxious visual material such as child abuse and extreme violence that could be damaging to mental health;
4. the practitioner had an independent line of management and accountability in the event that there was a perceived conflict with the investigational team, for example, if the practitioner believed that they were being subjected to pressure to find a certain result.

Other risks of bias include base rate expectations due to prior poor experience that leads to a bias away from the investigational hypothesis. For example, a previous experience of an inability to extract evidence from a particular type of device will possibly lessen the priority of analysis of a similar device when encountered in future investigations. Some of the mitigating countermeasures that can be used in digital forensics can include (1) training of digital forensic practitioners in cognitive psychology that is both practical and scenario based and that will enable practitioners to understand and experience how bias can occur; (2) testing and eliminating multiple competing hypotheses in an investigation of the same data and information; and (3) peer review processes that involve blind verification, which should be applied to both negative results and positive results.

The risks of bias affecting analysis and interpretation are real, but further research into the prevalence and impact of bias in digital forensics should be conducted. One potential remedy that has been proposed includes the removal of irrelevant case information, such as might be found in the case file, or the presence of a confession, or the personal opinions of the investigator about the suspect. Such information can be withheld by the investigator. However, the digital forensic examiner will encounter much more information concerning the case and the parties to the case than counterparts working in other forensic disciplines. The total information concerning the case, or a substantial majority of relevant information, will be present within the evidence that is processed and under analysis. That evidence will include documents, communications, images and videos that include personal details plus information that is not relevant to the case. For the examiner to undertake the examination efficiently and effectively, the examiner needs to understand the context of the case and to know what the investigation concerns, i.e. the activity that is suspected and the offences that are believed to have been committed. For example, is it an investigation into child exploitation in which the examiner is looking for relevant images, or does the investigation concern a sudden death such as an apparent homicide, or complex investigation into the planning of a terrorist attack involving multiple persons and locations? Contextual information such as scenarios and relevant dates and times is important for the examiner to conduct an appropriate search. While there exist sound arguments for providing the examiner with little to no context, the absence of context is an impracticable proposition. An analagous situation would be to present oneself to a medical doctor but without providing the doctor with any information by which they could begin an examination. Essentially, in answer to the doctor's question 'what is ailing you?' without providing any context, the patient would reply 'you tell me'.

In conflict with the need to mitigate the impact of any bias, due to the nature and volume of material encountered in a digital forensic investigation, examinations will necessarily be customised to deal with the circumstances of that particular case. Any potential bias can be managed and mitigated if the examiner records and reports the scope of the search including terms, phrases, file types, etc. and the contextual information that was provided to the examiner prior to and during the examination process.

The fallibility of human reasoning provides a strong incentive for following a scientific approach when analysing digital and multimedia evidence in a forensic context. Scientific practices, such as those used in digital evidence, cannot eliminate error, but the risks of error can be mitigated. The scientific method employs scientific reasoning, which can be described as abductive, deductive and inductive reasoning which is, sometimes, referred to as the hypothetico-deductive model. The National Institute of Standards and Technology describes abductive reasoning as '...eliminates implausible explanations and retains the most plausible explanation for (limited) available facts and traces, drawing analogies from past experience' [4], p. 3. Deductive reasoning tests the most plausible explanation against the observable traces with a focus on contradictory facts. If contradictory traces are found, the most plausible explanation must then be revised. Inductive reasoning can lead to knowledge specific to a set of circumstances and, therefore, provides trustworthy decision-making. Inductive reasoning can also lead to a generalised theory based on the observations of a number of circumstances, which provides new knowledge to forensic science [4].

Scientific reasoning is applied at different stages of the justice process. During the investigative phase, practitioners develop scenarios that explain the evidence, search for contradictory and predicted facts and interpret available information to arrive at a decision. As testimony is being prepared, practitioners consider the claims of the various parties to the litigation against the evidence of the traces, including looking for alternative explanations. Importantly and seemingly at odds with other actors within the justice system, scientific reasoning leads to probabilistic conclusions, not absolutism. Scientific reasoning arrives at a likely outcome given the available information, but that information might be limited, subject to cognitive bias and to influence by external factors such fatigue, a stressful or toxic work environment and personal distraction.

Science does not stand still and it is an ever growing body of knowledge. When the principles of scientific reasoning, as described earlier, are extended, into forensic science, it supports the fundamental principle of forensic science that experts' opinions should not be expressed as fact. Moreover, focusing on a single hypothesis could be an indication of bias or a failure to consider alternative possibilities, which then devalues the reliability of the evidence. For example, evidence of geolocation information had been presented in a particular case. The presiding judge was concerned, however, that the prosecution had failed to demonstrate that the underlying science of geolocation services had gained general acceptance in the relevant scientific community and that alternative hypotheses that might explain the evidence had not been considered [5]. Similar challenges have also been encountered in cases involving cell site analysis, where the evidence had been presented as predictable and factual, whereas such evidence is variable and subject to change over time due to several factors. Consequently the UK Forensic Science Regulator has included additional clauses in the Codes of Conduct for Digital Forensics–Cell Site Analysis that require practitioners to consider additional hypotheses; the terminology of the reports shall imply no bias so phrases such as 'in the vicinity of' and 'consistent with' can only be used with caveats. Further, limitations are placed on the use of cell site analysis as evidence that is used to form any hypotheses or investigative leads [6].

The previous paragraph highlights the growing expectation that digital traces are to be treated in a similar manner to that of forensic science more broadly, that is, evaluating and expressing the relative probabilities of two mutually exclusive hypotheses. In support of this approach, the Organisation of Scientific Area Committees published 'A Framework for Harmonizing Forensic Science Practices and Digital/Multimedia Evidence' to define the core forensic concepts and processes in the context of digital and multimedia evidence [4]. Simply put the forensic practitioner's responsibility is to focus on the digital traces, not to prove or disprove a specific claim. Subjectivity is involved in the evaluation of forensic findings, which is the responsibility of the judge and jury to consider the evidence and weigh it against all other information at the court's disposal to arrive at a verdict.

In the case of digital evidence, for example, when considering the recovery of a deleted file, forensic practitioners must consider whether the deleted file was recovered correctly and represents the actual, original contents of the deleted file. Importantly the deleted file recovery operations usually involve an estimation of what data were allocated to the deleted file, rather than a perfect copy of the file itself. It is, therefore, necessary for forensic practitioners to consider alternative hypotheses. Increasingly, in the United States and in Europe, forensic practitioners are expected to express the probability of the evidence given one claim versus an opposing claim.

To assist the finders of fact to understand the results of forensic examination, the forensic expert should not advocate for a specific outcome. Bias can influence the presentation of digital evidence, especially when the stakes are high, resulting in an inappropriate conveyance to the strength of the hypothesis that favours the client in an adversarial situation. Steps must be taken to prevent forensic practitioners from acting as advocates. This can be accomplished by insisting that the practitioner's evaluation of the evidence and expression of the results is in terms of the relative probabilities of evidence given at least two alternative claims. The alternative claims should be represented in the examiner's case notes and made available to counsel via the process determined by the rules of the jurisdiction.

Each of the phases of digital forensic examination (evidence identification, preservation, analysis and reporting) involves significant human involvement and is, therefore, vulnerable to the variabilities of human beings as outlined in this chapter. Each phase can be compromised by a suboptimal attention to quality, which will consequently lessen the reliability of the evidence. A significant impact on the quality of digital forensics for each of the main processes results from the pressure to reduce costs, a constant state of affairs in many, if not most, organisations, especially those in the public sector. For example, in some jurisdictions, untrained, or barely trained police officers are downloading data from mobile phones and presenting very superficial interpretations as evidence, which can be misleading and quite wrong. Or worse, phones are conveyed to the local mobile phone shop for downloading, then the results are being interpreted by inadequately trained officers. As the officer is often untrained, the data can be immediately misinterpreted; for example, automatically downloaded key words are mistaken for search terms or are interpreted without context [7].

As is clear from the issues identified in this chapter, human factors are greatly influenced by organisational culture, which, in turn, is underpinned by the articulated and practiced ethical and professional framework of the organisation. This applies not only to the digital evidence team but also to those who manage and lead the team, the division within which it is administratively structured, and, just as importantly, it also applies to the customers who are often internal customers and who may have a specific outcome in mind. On occasions, even in the most ethical of organisations, there can be a difference in understanding of the role of the digital evidence team. Some individuals might view the purpose of the digital evidence capability as one to support the customer to, for example, secure a prosecution of a suspect. Without strong leadership across the organisation, this might have the effect of shaping the behaviour, conduct and work of individual examiners. It should, at all times, be borne in mind that a professional, exemplary and comprehensive digital evidence examination might or might not identify evidence that supports the preferred claims of the investigator.

References

[1] N. Sunde, I. Dror, Cognitive and human factors in digital forensics: problems challenges, and the way forward, Digit. Investig. 29 (2019) 101–108.

[2] N. Sunde, Nontechnical sources of errors when handling digital evidence within a criminal investigation (Masters Thesis), The Faculty of Technology and Electrical Engineering, Norwegian University of Science and Technology, Sunde N. Gjovik, 2017.

[3] I. Dror, Human expert performance in forensic decision-making: seven different sources of bias, Aust. J. Forensic Sci. 49 (5) (2017) 541–547.

[4] NIST, A Framework for Harmonizing Forensic Science Practices and Digital/Multimedia Evidence, National Institutes of Standards and Testing: Organization of Scientific Area Committees for Forensic Science, 2018. Retrieved from https://www.nist.gov/sites/default/files/documents/2018/01/10/osac_ts_0002.pdf.

[5] E. Casey, Editorial: clearly conveying digital forensic results, Digit. Investig. 24 (2018) 1–3.

[6] Forensic Science Regulator, Codes of practice appendix: digital forensics – cell site analysis, 2016, Issue 1. Retrieved from https://assets.publishing.service.gov.uk/government/uploads/system/uploads/attachment_data/file/528197/FSR-C-135_Cell_Site_Analysis_Issue_1.pdf.

[7] J. Collie, Commentary: digital forensic evidence – flaws in the criminal justice system, Forensic Sci. Int. 289 (2018) 154–155.

Tool validation

10

There exists considerable disagreement within the digital forensic community on the subject of tool validation. It should not be inferred from this chapter that tool vendors are producing substandard tools but, rather, that there are issues that need to be addressed concerning the validation of tools and processes that are used to examine digital traces. Digital forensic tools are used to identify evidence regarding the guilt or innocence of persons accused of having committed a crime and for which the potential penalties are severe. If the evidence is incorrect due to tool error, the innocent might be incarcerated, the guilty might be free to reoffend and certainly the reputation of the examiner and employer will be damaged, possibly irretrievably beyond repair.

As is the case with consumer and business software, it is well understood that flaws exist in digital forensic software. Some flaws are of a severity that they can impact on an investigation with the affect and consequences of unreliable tools leading to the possibility of inaccurate evidence that, in turn, impacts the client and the practitioner. In the United Kingdom the Forensic Science Regulator requires digital forensic laboratories to obtain ISO 17025 accreditation that emphasises the demonstrable development and effective implementation of adequate testing and validation methods. The regulator has developed guidelines that embed validation into laboratory practices by which accreditation can be achieved. The digital forensic examiner usually commences their analysis following the preservation and acquisition phase which is performed by the forensic software. The acquisition phase is not manually verifiable, but is instead confirmed by signals provided by the forensic tools that are made visually accessible to the examiner [1, 2].

Three error types can be encountered in digital forensics: (1) tool errors in which the forensic software misinterprets or misrepresents the data, (2) tool limitation errors in defining the scope in which the software can be expected to perform and (3) user errors in which the software is used in a way for which it was not designed. Tools errors can occur in several ways including accidental errors, errors in software updates, software rot (the deterioration of software over time), inadvertent and intentional bias and flawed self-test diagnostics. Detecting tool errors in digital forensics can be especially fraught with risk as there is little opportunity for manual validation of the results due to the inability to touch or view the evidence and the contents of a device cannot be viewed without compromising data integrity. The discipline is in the position where it must verify and validate its tools by using the tools themselves, therefore finding itself in an infinite loop. Consequently the field tends to fall into an environment of recognising certain tools as industry standards which defaults to an assumption based on the widespread opinion of multiple practitioners. The risk of this approach is to fall into an environment of group think, from which no person or professional can be certain that they are immune. Should an examiner believe that they are immune from group think in such circumstances, then other, more significant issues of cognitive bias are

Strategic Leadership in Digital Evidence. https://doi.org/10.1016/B978-0-12-819618-2.00010-3

present which is discussed elsewhere in this volume. Further, examiners will have a tendency to stay with the tools with which they are familiar, almost forming a fan base as happens with a sporting team resulting in an emotional faith in their favourite tools and the vendors. This can lead to close mindedness when a tool is not performing as it purports to or failure to recognise when a tool update does not meet the requirements of a new version of consumer application that is under analysis.

As tool validation is difficult, dual tooling, using the tools of different vendors or suppliers, is often used to substitute for verification and validation. This approach improves the chances of reliability, but it does not provide a guarantee. Therefore tools that are used for the identification and interpretation of well-documented artefacts have been subjected to long-term research and scrutiny are generally accepted. However, artefacts associated with new and emerging technology are promoted as being 'supported' by tool manufacturers, but the algorithm development and testing are invisible to users, meaning that the extent of the testing for variables and reproducibility cannot be objectively and independently assessed.

Vendors and authoritative forensic expert groups advise that tools should be tested and validated by users before being applied to case work. However, some practitioners, erroneously, do not consider this to be part of the practitioner's role. This view is despite most examiners holding the belief that the current state of forensic tool testing is unsatisfactory. Part of the examiner's role is to engage in the court process and, therefore, adhere to the evidence admissibility and reliability governance which explicitly requires test and validation of the tools that they use. It is incumbent on examiners to know, understand and be confident in the tools that they use. If examiners choose to absent themselves from the testing and validation requirements, they are, in effect, not fulfilling their obligations to the court to which they attest when presenting testimony. If an examiner is not fulfilling their obligations, they are failing any test of ethical conduct and any claim that they might make to expertise is false. The evidence presented by digital forensic examiners in criminal matters must meet the standard of 'beyond reasonable doubt', which is a high burden of proof. If the examiner cannot guarantee that an examination is based on a reliable representation of the suspect material, then it is subject to a reasonable doubt. The inability to guarantee the required validity raises some valid questions for defence counsel: (1) why has the tool not been able to effectively acquire data, (2) what has the tool missed and (3) what has a tool potentially added? [3]

Although the distinction between each type of error is clear, categorising an error as one type or another can be more difficult. The default settings of many forensic tools are 'dumbed down' to allow for a wider population of users which can then lead to inadvertent misuse of the tool. If the practitioner's knowledge is lacking, it can lead to misinterpretation of the evidence regarding a particular event. For example, a tool may purport to recover Internet history, but what are the limitations of this recovery with variables such as browser type, version and settings and search engine type, as the version and settings are among some variables that could impact on the performance of the tool. If the practitioner is unaware of any limitations, can the error be classified as a tool error, a user error or a lack of transparency and documentation from the vendor?

End-user licence agreements for digital forensics set out the responsibilities and liabilities for vendors and users. In general terms, end-user licence agreements offer no guarantee that digital forensic software will be error free or operate without interruption. Further the licence agreements state that the user assumes all risk in using the software and that users will not disclose any results of testing or performance to any third party. Clearly the liability lies with the practitioner to establish the reliability of the tools that they use.

Software updates, including bug fixes, are released from time to time along with vendors' advice detailing changes in the updates. It is, therefore, reasonable to assume that a tool, when previously applied to a given case in certain circumstances, was operating in error. Organisations should, with the benefit of this hindsight knowledge, review historic cases to determine if the previous version of the tool that was applied to those cases was operating in error for those elements that were subject to examination. Such historic case review could reveal additional evidence or reinterpret previously found evidence with the benefit of the update.

Although the commercial interests of the tool vendors are served by nondisclosure of user testing and performance results, this restriction on publishing tool performance data negatively impacts the discipline's pursuit of reliability. As the only recourse of those who do test their tools is to report back to the vendors themselves, it prevents the timely dissemination to other users that they might also take remedial actions. Further, testers who identify an error may be less motivated to report the error at all and might just establish a local work around which will leave other users vulnerable to unknowingly repeating the error. In addition, reporting an error without reward, in the form of compensation or recognition from peers, may disincentivise testing work which would result in the testing work not being undertaken.

There was considerable attention paid to tool testing in the period 2007–12 that resulted in several papers in the academic and industry literature. During and since that period, the National Institute of Standards and Technology has implemented a tool testing programme, and the Scientific Working Group on Digital Evidence and the Organisation for Scientific Area Committees have turned their attention to standards in digital evidence. However, there is little discussion as to whether the tools are demonstrably trustworthy. Also the programmes have some shortcomings, most notably the significant time lag between the release of a version of a tool, the testing of that specific version and subsequent publication of testing results, and the often narrow scope of testing, testing protocols and user preferences which does not reflect the wide variety of situations that are encountered in case work.

There are a number of potential solutions to solve the issues of tool validation. A formalised tool error/tool limitation discovery repository could be established for all users to contribute. The courts, possibly through the office of prosecutors, could seek improved procedural and testing disclosures. The vendors could take responsibility for improved functionality disclosures, test data disclosures, alerts and error handling (e.g. in addition to release updates that note additional support, release updates of terminated support would also be helpful). Organisational leadership and management of external factors such as practitioner competence and the prioritisation of speed over quality could mitigate the impact of tool errors. The challenge for public disclosure of tool errors and limitations, however, could be exploited by those engaging in contrary conduct.

The NIST Federated Testing programme that is conducted through the cooperation of multiple agencies and countries could make a substantial contribution to addressing the current deficiency. It is noted that it is impossible to test all scenarios in which a tool will be applied. Even when considering a single function of the tool, there are multiple valid outcomes with variables contained within. Testing and verification of tools are yet to reach the threshold of factual accuracy of their functions, which is exacerbated by the continual release of updates to existing tools and the release of new tools [2]. Whatever external centralised and group processes are employed to test and monitor digital forensics tool performance, the examiner is not excused from informing him/herself and being fully knowledgeable of a tool vulnerabilities.

As digital forensics has moved from the situation of analysis of data that is resident on physical devices to that where data is acquired from other locations and subsequently analysed, new vulnerabilities to the reliability of the process have emerged. For example, the humble write blocker, which has been a reliable mainstay of digital forensics since the beginnings of the field, prevents writing to the target media during the acquisition process. The principle of the write blocker is extended to situations where data is acquired from networks and the cloud. Without being too technical, advances in digital forensics include the ability to remotely image a drive on a disk of interest across a network which is dependent on the ability to browse drives that are attached to the write blocker via the Internet Small Computer System Interface (iSCSI) protocol. The iSCSI can command the SCSI to be delivered over local area networks, wide area networks and the Internet. Since the target drive can be imaged remotely, security testing should be integrated into the process of testing digital forensic tools to ensure the reliability of the process. Without security testing and assurance, users could potentially be created and modified, and their settings altered, with these systems. The risk to the write blocking process, when security testing has not been conducted, can be demonstrated through a compromise to the destination drive by altering a warning message that can, for example, obfuscate the compromise. With relative ease, an adversary could substitute a compromised firmware update for a genuine update and convince the digital forensic practitioner to unknowingly install the compromised version. The possibility of this situation is exacerbated by the lack of training in cyber security and foundational computer education and training for many law enforcement digital forensic examiners. In another example of potential compromise using cybersecurity techniques, although hash values are the accepted authentication of the duplication of digital traces, the generation of the hash value can also be compromised so that the duplication appears to be authentic. It is recommended that digital forensic examiners should integrate security testing into the forensic tool testing process [4].

To conclude the digital forensic field is under a legal and ethical obligation to improve its standards, and therefore, every opportunity for improvement should be taken. As more tool testing is undertaken, the higher likelihood it is that tool errors will be identified and that reliability will be improved. Improved, cooperative and shared tool testing will only serve to improve outcomes for those involved in the justice system and disputation. Lastly, if comprehensive validation of a tool's functionality is infeasible, then testing of those functions where the risk of error is greater in terms of frequency and severity should receive the highest priority and immediate attention.

References

[1] G. Horsman, "I couldn't find it your honour, it mustn't be there!" – tool errors, tool limitations and user error in digital forensics, Sci. Justice 58 (2018) 433–440.

[2] G. Horsman, Tool testing and reliability issues in the field of digital forensics, Digit. Investig. 28 (2019) 163–175.

[3] Scientific Working Group on Digital Evidence, SWGDE Establishing Confidence in Digital and Multimedia Evidence Forensic Results by Error Mitigation Analysis, Retrieved from, https://www.swgde.org/documents/Current%20Documents/SWGDE%20Establishing%20Confidence%20in%20Digital%20Forensic%20Results%20by%20Error%20Mitigation%20Analysis, 2018.

[4] C. Meffert, I. Baggili, F. Breitinger, Deleting collected digital evidence by exploiting a widely adopted hardware write blocker, Digit. Investig. 18 (2016) S87–S96.

Datasets

11

The use of datasets can be an important aid in research, for example, in the construction of an email parser, malware analysis, improve specific purpose algorithms or for the testing of tools. For datasets to be useful, they must possess three features: (1) quality to ensure that results are accurate and generalizable, (2) quantity to ensure that there are sufficient data to train and validate the tools and (3) availability for the research to be conducted and independently reproduced to ensure scientific validity. Further, funding agencies increasingly require that grantees make the results of their research available to the public. The current deficiencies in most databases that fail to meet these criteria present major weaknesses in assuring the reliability of research and testing and to the continued development in digital forensics. The majority of test databases are deficient as (1) many researchers produced their own datasets, (2) datasets are not released after the work has been completed and (3) there is a lack of labelled standardised datasets that can be used in research. These weaknesses lead to the disadvantages of low reproducibility, comparability and peer-validated research [1]. Over half the datasets used to conduct published research were experiment generated, where researchers created specific scenarios to conduct their experiments due to the lack of available real-world datasets and datasets that have been created specifically to conduct experiments on new technology.

User-generated datasets, that is, real-world datasets, are crucial for developing reliable algorithms and tools. However, sharing can be inhibited by copyright protections and privacy law. A prominent example of a real-world dataset is the Enron email dataset, which was posted online by the Federal Energy Regulatory Commission and later purchased by the Massachusetts Institute of Technology. It has become a de facto standard for research and for tool performance measurement. Private user information and email attachments were removed to avoid violating privacy rights. Some institutions collect real-world information, for example, from students who have signed an agreement for researchers to capture the information. Some datasets have been generated through collaboration between law enforcement and academia, while other data are publicly available online. In addition, the National Institutes of Standards and Technology hosts collections such as the National Software Reference Library and the National Vulnerability Database. Computer-generated datasets are the smallest category of datasets.

References

[1] C. Grajeda, F. Breitinger, I. Baggili, Availability of datasets for digital forensics—and what is missing, Digit. Investig. 11 (2017) S94–S105.

Strategic Leadership in Digital Evidence. https://doi.org/10.1016/B978-0-12-819618-2.00011-5

The risks for digital evidence

12

After the discussion of quality assurance in digital evidence, the question of the future naturally follows. Some leaders in the field have made the disturbing observation that the overall quality of digital forensic examination is declining, and the comprehension of cybercrime is diminishing. This reliable observation appears to be in conflict with the simultaneous improvement in the general public's knowledge of technology and its attendant utility irrespective of the level of economic development. Further, such a decline is occurring at a time when all communities are becoming more dependent on technology and therefore individuals are generating more digital traces representing the thoughts, behaviours and actions that might be used in evidence in any proceedings. This decline is a great concern as the consequences of errors and omissions in forensic science result in miscarriages of justice, and dangerous criminals will continue to be at large to perpetrate further crimes against persons and organisations [1]. The public rightfully expects that its justice system will continuously improve in meeting the needs of the community and to have confidence in the evidence that might be presented.

The increasing quantity, diversity, diffusion, structural intricacy and complexity in the use of data, sometimes referred to as the oil of the 21st century, make it increasingly difficult for the digital forensic examiner to find the most investigatively useful information. Attorneys and judges are struggling to learn how to evaluate and interpret digital forensic results and the intimate and detailed nature of digital traces raises privacy concerns that must be considered in all stages of the data preservation, examination and reporting processes.

The situation is further compounded by competing demands to follow methodical, scientific practices and to respond in shorter time frames yet deal with the dual challenges of growth in cybercrime and the increasing volume of data in the lake. In addition, organisations and first responders are increasing their demand for decentralised forensic capabilities (e.g. at the crime scene) and for correlation capabilities to identify emerging trends and seriality. The calls on digital evidence are multiple and complex.

In its early history, digital forensic practitioners considered the data from devices as fact-based evidence with little consideration given to evaluation of alternative interpretations. This approach still persists today to a significant degree with the effect of denying the scientific basis to the field. To this day, there is still a significant volume of debate about what aspects of digital forensics are or are not science and some forensic science publications still do not recognise digital forensics as a forensic discipline.

The risks in digital forensics are adequately addressed as technical and interpretive errors which, therefore, continue to be ongoing challenges. Practitioners generally have an inadequate understanding of the operation of hardware and software that leads to a flawed interpretation of the analysis of data. Consequently, practitioners rely heavily on tools to process data without due regard to the limitations and inherent errors within the tools. The inadequate understanding of practitioners resulting in the

Strategic Leadership in Digital Evidence. https://doi.org/10.1016/B978-0-12-819618-2.00012-7

consequent overreliance on commercial tools and vendor training is exacerbated by the highly dynamic technical and operational environments of rapidly evolving technology and the increased prevalence of digital technology used in the conduct of criminal activity. There are numerous cases where incorrect conclusions, false accusations and misinterpretation of data have led to poor investigational and court outcomes.

Treating the field as fact based, rather than a scientific discipline, is useful in certain circumstances. It is useful when the data are to be used as information to assist in investigations, including developing the investigation hypothesis and subsequent fact checking. It is also useful to locate additional data sources or to find potential suspects or victims. Given that digital traces can be altered or parsed incorrectly by the tools and digital forensic results can be open to interpretation and, therefore, misinterpretation, the assumption that digital forensics is based on fact is dangerous, especially when used as evidence rather than investigative information or for intelligence. Some courts have recognised that digital forensics is not fact-based evidence and have questioned the validity of digital forensic reports due to the absence of demonstrable scientific validity in the analytical process.

The future risks to digital forensics arise in several areas including, but not limited to:

- Application to many contexts including investigations, military, critical infrastructure protection and intelligence operations, with each context treating digital evidence differently and developing context-specific standard procedures. To transfer knowledge and processes from one context to another, for example, from an intelligence purpose to a criminal investigation purpose, without due consideration can lead to a flawed interpretation of findings.
- Decentralisation, including the deployment of advanced digital forensic techniques by persons with limited knowledge, can result in errors and the lost opportunities for broader visibility across the crime environment and to compare multiple crimes. Forensic intelligence is a function of forensic science that is becoming increasingly favoured by many organisations, with some excellent results being realised. Digital forensics lends itself very well to a forensic intelligence function, but if examinations are being conducted in a decentralised environment, it is unlikely that the data will be captured in the consolidated repository and merged with other forensic information, therefore it will be unavailable to fulfil the intelligence function.
- Dynamism of the field with new technology and devices, such as the Internet of Things, outpaces the scientists' ability to understand the new technology that they are likely to encounter in case work.
- Growth in case and data volumes continues at massive rates that greatly outstrips the capacity of organisations to manage and to adjust. For most organisations, the ability to purchase digital forensics tools and equipment is compromised as it is often referred to as 'computer equipment' or similar and is therefore subject to organisation- or government-wide procurement policies, including approval by the IT manager. The requirement to follow such processes compromises the ability of digital forensic teams to respond to emerging issues and can comprise the selection of best fit for purpose.
- Knowledge management and information sharing within the digital forensics community and between groups within the justice system and only sporadically applied within forensic organisations.

- Poor quality management with many of the processes used in digital forensics occurring outside of a quality framework that increases the risk of errors and omissions.
- Privacy is, rightly, becoming an increasing concern. Governments and businesses can access huge amounts of personal and private data, but the tension between privacy and digital forensics is complex. Recent examples include the ongoing tension between the US Department of Justice, who seeks a 'backdoor' to Apple's iPhone encryption while Apple seeks to maintain a secure device for its users; and, the promotion of tracking and contact apps by the governments of several countries as a part of their response to COVID-19, but concern by citizens that it is a movement towards a permanent state of surveillance. Ignoring privacy concerns of the community at large may result in the limitation of utility of digital evidence through the means of regulation and legislation.

Some steps are being taken to address the risks. The United States Scientific Working Group on Digital Evidence (SWGDE) has developed an error mitigation approach that will identify each potential source of error encompassing technology and human factors. There is some overlap with ISO 17020 and ISO 17025 that are used for the basis of forensic accreditation. It is important to emphasise that error mitigation analysis involves testing and validation of digital forensic tools, but it does not deal with the evaluation of evidence and mitigation of bias.

Work is being undertaken to harmonise forensic science and digital forensics. The Digital Media Scientific Area Committee (of the National Institute of Standards and Technology, Organisation of Scientific Area Committees) has developed a forensic science framework for digital traces with a view to it being applied to other disciplines. The framework is based on scientific reasoning that addresses defined questions of authentication, identification, classification, reconstruction and evaluation in a broad range of legal contexts.

To mitigate the risk created by the potential loss of knowledge in digital forensics, knowledge management strategies can be implemented:

- The scope of forensic examination can be determined by the purpose to which it is being applied and then conducted to the extent that is appropriate for that purpose. Generally speaking, there are three tiers of forensic examination that are applied (triage, preliminary examination and in-depth examination) in practice which will indicate the extent of resources that are to be directed to the task at hand.
- Digital forensic knowledge can be codified in automated solutions.
- The gigital forensic community can construct a collaborative knowledge exchange including multidisciplinary conferences and structured knowledge management systems (such as instructional documents and videos).
- Organisations can designate forensic advisors, who specialise in digital forensics, to liaise with and guide investigators and to provide appropriate contextual information for examiners.
- Forensic intelligence teams that specialise in digital forensics.
- Interoperability and automation, for example, the ability to combine the results of multiple tools that are used to extract information from all data sources will significantly improve the efficiency and effectiveness of an investigation and facilitate verification and the sharing of information.

Several initiatives are under development in multiple organisations including the support of forensic intelligence capabilities. Organisations will continue to be challenged as some of the developments in digital forensic capabilities are progressing at a pace that far exceeds that at which forensic science can adapt [1].

Reference

[1] E. Casey, The chequered past and risky future of digital forensics, Aust. J. Forensic Sci. 51 (6) (2019) 649–664.

Sources of data

13

The information technology industry continues to develop and innovate new technologies that are made available to the business and consumer markets. These innovations lead to an increasing range of devices, systems and locations from which probative data can be obtained. Each new technology, each new offering from a vendor and each new device represents a unique challenge to the examiner.

Cloud storage forensics

Cloud computing services have recently emerged as a significant issue for digital forensic examiners and investigations. Cloud computing comprises three broad categories of services:

1. Software as a service (SaaS) whereby an application accesses the shared infrastructure of the cloud storage provider, for example, in storage as a service.
2. Platform as a service (PaaS) in which the user deploys and runs applications on the cloud storage provider's infrastructure.
3. Infrastructure as a service (IaaS) whereby the underlying computer resources, such as the operating system or other software, are provided by the cloud storage provider.

It was anticipated that 95% of companies will use an SaaS business model in the foreseeable future, with 83% using PaaS and 73% using IaaS [1]. The SaaS market alone is expected to reach $157 billion in 2020 [2] (Table 13.1).

Conducting analysis of data stored in the cloud presents new challenges that are unlike those of traditional and even mobile forensics. Cloud computing forensic science is defined as '…the application of scientific principles, technological practices and derived and proven methods to reconstruct past cloud computing events through identification, collection, preservation, examination, interpretation and reporting of digital evidence'. [3]

The National Institute of Standards and Technology identified 65 specific challenges to performing forensic investigations in the cloud:

- architecture—diversity, complexity, provenance, multitenancy and data segregation
- data collection—data integrity, data recovery, data location and imaging
- analysis—correlation, reconstruction, time synchronisation, logs, metadata and timelines
- antiforensics—obfuscation, data hiding and malware
- incident first response—trustworthiness of cloud providers, response time and reconstruction
- role management—data owners, identity management, users and access control
- legal—jurisdictions, laws, service level agreements, contracts, subpoenas, international cooperation, privacy and ethics
- standards—standard operating procedures, interoperability, testing and validation
- training—forensic investigators, cloud providers, qualification and certification.

Strategic Leadership in Digital Evidence. https://doi.org/10.1016/B978-0-12-819618-2.00013-9

Table 13.1 Distinction between various cloud services.

Traditional On-Premises IT	Colocation	Hosting	Infrastructure-as-a-Service	Platform-as-a-Service	Software-as-a-Service
Data	Data	Data	Data	Data	Data
Application	Application	Application	Application	Application	Application
Databases	Databases	Databases	Databases	Databases	Databases
Operating System	Operating System	Operating System	Operating System	Operating System	Operating System
Virtualisation	Virtualisation	Virtualisation	Virtualisation	Virtualisation	Virtualisation
Hardware Servers	Hardware Servers	Hardware Servers	Hardware Servers	Hardware Servers	Hardware Servers
Network and Storage	Network and Storage	Network and Storage	Network and Storage	Network and Storage	Network and Storage
Data Centre	Data Centre	Data Centre	Data Centre	Data Centre	Data Centre

Provider Managed | Self Managed

Most of the research in conducting cloud forensic investigations has been undertaken in the past 3–4 years [4]. Cloud forensic examiners are trying to keep up with not only updates to devices and software but also to changes made to software and hardware made by end users.

The traditional model of digital forensics is client (device) centric in which the examiner works with physical evidence devices, such as computers, storage media or mobile devices including smartphones. Digital forensics, therefore, was focused on the physical location of the computation and the storage of the data. The underlying assumption was that most data are local. Gmail became the first mass used web application. In the software as a service cloud model, both the code (software) and the data are delivered over the network on demand. Consequently, in cloud computing the local storage, for example, hard drive, performs the function of a cache and not that of the data repository as it does in traditional digital forensics [5].

Several different approaches have been developed to address the challenges of digital forensics in cloud computing. One approach is the development of new tools specifically for the purpose of forensic examination of cloud storage, including (1) using the service providers' API[a] to perform a complete acquisition of the drive's content, (2) study how web apps store and work with artefacts, (3) using a file system interface to the cloud drive to bridge the semantic gap between cloud artefacts and legacy tools,

[a] An API (Application Programming Interface) is a set of functions and procedures that allow the creation of applications that access the features or data of an operating system, application, or other service, and allows third parties to use the functionality of that software application.

(4) rewinding the state of the drive as of a particular time, (5) identification of all recorded activity between two points in time and (6) filtering drive data based on the metadata provided by the cloud services.

A fundamental difference when conducting forensics in the cloud in comparison to client-centric analysis, is that many of the required investigative functions are already present in the cloud systems. Software development practices have changed to one where functionality can be composed from autonomous modules that communicate over APIs and distributed between clients and servers. One result of these practices is that routine logging routinely records user input; therefore the historical information is already present and the cloud service itself can be directed to efficiently and reliably reveal it.

The shift from the client centric software as a product to cloud computing's software as a service changes the fundamental concepts of digital forensics that have been in place since the field's inception. The traditional doctrine of acquiring data from physical devices does not translate well the SaaS world as it can be demonstrably incomplete, and, at times, it can also be false. If one is to perform best practice forensic science and seek to obtain the best evidence, it follows that the investigative focus should be to obtain the most authoritative data source which, in the case of cloud computing, is that evidence which is stored in the cloud.

As businesses and consumers move more of their IT requirements to cloud services, forensic examiners will be increasingly called upon to examine data in cloud environments. A word of caution is appropriate though as, while cloud infrastructure and services might appear to be similar irrespective of the provider, there are substantial differences in the architecture and functionality of cloud services between providers, including between the offerings of the same provider as they optimise infrastructure and services for specific business functions. This is especially so at the API level even if the APIs purportedly perform similar functions. To meet the changes presented by the cloud environment, forensic practitioners will require additional skills including the ability to write case-specific solutions that can perform acquisitions using APIs. Further, it is likely that, due to the rapidly increasing volume of cloud-stored data and the associated logistical problems with moving and/or copying the data to an examiner managed environment, one possible solution will be to forward deploy forensic tools to the cloud where the forensic analysis will be conducted.

While the earlier comments were based on experiments that sought solutions to the challenges of cloud computing forensics in the environments of well-known SaaS providers, it is estimated that there are between 200 and 300 commercial cloud service providers in the world today. Each provider will have its own design strategy and architecture(s) specific to the business models that it supports. Substantial, but by no means exhaustive, research has been conducted by a number of groups who have looked at a variety of commercial offerings. For example, in one study, the forensic implications of the cloud storage environments of three providers (SpiderOak, JustCloud and pCloud) were examined. Users of the three cloud services can download, upload and access their data using a web browser and a client application, such as a specific app which is also available on mobile devices. Other functionalities that might also be available, depending on the provider and the means of access (browser or app) include, but are not necessarily limited to, file creation, scheduling and restoration of backups; sharing files with or without password-protected links; syncing across devices; encryption of all cloud stored data; the ability to upload data by other users who have account access; and perform backups from other services including social media [6].

Detailed forensic observations and findings of the client devices were made for each of the three cloud providers, including (1) account creation, (2) cloud application programme, (3) uninstalling the cloud application programme, (4) downloading from the cloud using the browser and (5) browsing and downloading from the respective cloud accounts. Various forensic artefacts were located when using Internet Explorer, Firefox and Google Chrome browsers, and the client application on Windows machines and iOS devices. The artefacts included email addresses, the identity and the name of the created account and the names of the uploaded and downloaded files. User credentials could also be recovered from memory. When downloaded from the cloud service, the files were identical to those that were uploaded as verified by the checksum values; however, the timestamp and some other data were subject to change.

Other researchers have also studied pCloud, a service that provides client-side encryption meaning that, as data leaves the client's system, it is encrypted. The experiments were to determine what data can be found on Windows, Ubuntu, Android and iOS operating systems when using pCloud; what data are leaked when using Google Chrome and Internet Explorer browsers on Windows operating systems; what data of forensic interest can be discovered in live memory and what data can be captured in network traffic? [7] Each of the browsers and operating systems revealed different artefacts. For example, in the Windows-based browser experiments, uploaded filenames and usernames could be revealed; and passwords, email addresses, filenames and directories were discoverable in physical memory as Internet Explorer saves pCloud credentials in the registry. Similarly, username and passwords could be found when Google Chrome was used as the browser. In the Android experiments, pCloud-specific folders were created, and a database containing usernames, email quota and tables related to pCloud communications could be found. Following deinstallation of the pCloud app, website information and cookies related to pCloud could be found in the memory.

Locating pCloud artefacts in the iOS experiments was more difficult than in the other experiments, and pCloud login details could not be found. Some other useful information could be found including 'session ID', 'API key', the pCloud installation directory location and uploaded filenames. Following uninstallation, some deleted files could be recovered. In contrast, in the Ubuntu experiments, many artefacts could be found in the memory including, importantly, the username and password. In addition, the uploaded filenames and file path could be obtained and after deletion of the files from the app, the username could be recovered from memory.

Other researchers studied the artefacts resulting from the use of a further selection of cloud providers (Cloud Me and 360Yunpan) operating in a range of browsers (Internet Explorer, Google Chrome and Mozilla Firefox) and client applications (Windows, Android and Apple iOS). CloudMe is a European cloud service that offers secure cloud storage, syncing of files and client software for managing cloud data across various devices. 360Yunpan is a Chinese cloud service notable for its huge (36 terabytes) of free storage space for users. Valuable forensic evidence could be found related to CloudMe and 360Yunpan storage accounts on various platforms. Digital traces included information related to user credentials, device names and filenames. The data could be found on hard drives, live memory, internal phone memory, backup files, network traffic and more [8].

To assist the process of forensic examinations of the cloud, some researchers have begun to attempt to elucidate a specific taxonomy. For example, artefacts of 31 free cloud apps that appear on an Android mobile device are assessed. Artefacts are usually found in the internal storage for some apps and comprise pictures, documents, audio files and web files. The artefacts informed the categorisation of the apps into three groups based on the retrieved files: (1) no recovered data, (2) database files only generated in internal storage but without file recovery and (3) database files and cloud-based data recovered [9].

The purpose of describing the detail of the earlier research is not for the reader to memorise the details of each combination of cloud service, device and browser or app. After all, it is unlikely that, if you are reading this book, you are going to be doing cloud forensic investigations and many of the more popular cloud services have not been included in the above experiments. Virtualisation technology, with the cloud being one form, has become increasingly prevalent and will continue to do so. To become proficient in the conduct of forensic investigations in virtual environments, examiners will require a thorough understanding of the environment, the storage of log files and the ability to access those files. The purpose is to provide some idea of the complexity and significant differences between systems that will impact on the ability to conduct an effective forensic examination of cloud data. The wide selection of cloud providers, together with the multiple combinations of devices, operating systems and browsers, without including any consideration of the user settings that have been selected, demonstrates the complexity of the task. For forensic analysts to conduct forensic investigations in cloud environments, the forensic examiner should have a thorough understanding of the cloud environment, the way in which logs are generated and stored and the way in which the data are structured and stored. As a leader of your digital evidence capability, the resources, training, skills and expectations will be informed by your understanding of this complexity.

Phone forensics

Devices

The purpose of this section is to provide the reader with a sense of the complexity, the diversity, variation and the range of issues that impact on mobile forensics, therefore impacting on the examination of mobile data. Although some technical detail is included, I do not envisage that the reader would want to remember the detail, although it has been simplified as much as possible without rendering it meaningless. Having an awareness of the issues will enable a leader to comprehend advice that might be provided by examiners, to be able to ask informed questions and to brief other members of the leadership team when providing situational updates or seeking resources. It should be borne in mind that, by the time that this volume is published, much of the technical detail alluded to will be obsolete. To stay abreast of contemporary knowledge, examiners will need to be given the space and time to effectively research and trial the most up-to-date information concerning the specific case that is under examination.

Mobile phones, broadly categorised into smartphones (essentially small, Internet-enabled computers that can make phone calls, text etc.) and feature phones (low-cost phones that are generally limited to calls and text and are often referred to, or used, as 'burner' phones) are now the most important device for digital evidence in law enforcement due to their ubiquity in people's lives. Mobile forensics has evolved as a subdiscipline of computer forensics which, therefore, did not focus on case domain information from mobile investigations. The growth in volume and complexity of mobile devices, especially smartphones, has grown substantially over the past decade, perhaps more so than any other area of consumer technology. The iOS (Apple) and Android (Samsung, Google etc.) operating systems are the most prevalent and have grown from an average storage of 16 GB in 2007 to 512 GB in 2017. Also, microSD card storage, used in some phones, has grown approximately 1000 times from 512 MB to 512 GB and SD cards from 1 GB to 1 TB over the same time period [10]. Generally speaking, existing mobile forensic models are based on proprietary solutions.

There are broadly two ways to acquire evidence from a phone, the physical and the logical acquisition.[b] The physical acquisition copies the device's entire data directly from the device's physical storage media such as the memory chip or flash storage by means of a bit-by-bit near exact copy. There are several approaches for undertaking a physical acquisition including direct connection to the intact device, physical chip extraction (commonly referred to as 'chip off') and Joint Test Action Group (JTAG).

The logical approach to acquisition is an image creation process facilitated by a copy of the logical objects such as files and folders from the data storage volumes. The weakness of this approach is that it only acquires logically allocated data, not a raw image and it generally does not recover deleted data. The logical acquisition requires that the phone is switched on, the operating system is loaded and it has the potential to overwrite the data stored in flash memory. The physical acquisition will usually obtain a more complete data set from the phone than the logical one and is more likely to include deleted data.

As the use of mobile phones continues to rapidly evolve, therefore, so do the forensic challenges. Emerging challenges for practitioners engaged in the examination of mobile phones include cloud applications, malware, mobile phones used as part of botnets and SCADA systems [11]. It has been well established that no single tool or technique recovers all data and therefore information of potential forensic interest

[b] The manual acquisition method has been ignored as it refers to the retrieval of data using the phone keypad and usually taking photos of the screen. Using the manual method compromises the integrity of the evidence as every interaction with the keypad writes new data to the memory.

from a device. Depending on the tool and phone combination, it is estimated that around 60%–70% of data can be recovered by a single tool, that is, if any can be recovered at all! Using a combination of tools can raise the total recovery rate by around 10%–20%. While it is apparent that, although the current suite of tools reflect close to current best practice, the subdiscipline of mobile forensics appears to be increasingly struggling to keep up with the rapid development in capability as reflected in the mobile device market.

The importance of mobile forensics continues to grow as mobile phones are a more affordable and convenient means of accessing the Internet for a significant proportion of users. In addition, there is a proliferation of mobile malware with users less likely to be able to recognise those threats in combination with poor cyber hygiene as users generally do not to manage their mobile security. This combination increases the attack surface for mobile devices. The challenge of mobile forensics is exacerbated by the proliferation of devices, systems and apps with the need for digital forensic practitioners to adhere to the principles of sound collection of evidence [12]. Understanding the behaviour of mobile device users can be useful to digital forensic examiners when conducting an examination. For example, QR codes have a useful and legitimate purpose that users have embraced; however, attackers have realised that they can also serve as a tool for redirection to fake websites and for the installation of malware onto user devices. In a social experiment, it has been found that the secure use of mobile phones is largely influenced by the cognitive impulsivity of the user. The possibility of exploiting possible remnants of user activities that resulted from user impulsivity and lack of knowledge could be included in the consideration and planning of mobile forensic investigations.

The digital forensic examination of local storage on mobile devices sets out to achieve three objectives: (1) what information is stored, (2) where the information is stored and (3) how the information is stored [13]. Dynamic analysis is the most common method for data acquisition, but it has several drawbacks including (1) it is hard to trigger all the paths of programmes that are or might be relevant to the investigation, which could result in criminal behaviour remaining undetected or the acquisition of content that is encoded or of unknown format rendering it very difficult to analyse and (2) manual reverse engineering, which is arduous and time consuming and, therefore, problematic if producing results are subject to time pressures.

SQLite is the most popular storage engine for messaging applications on mobile devices. Without straying into technical detail, phone manufacturers will use different types of encoding within the SQLite database.[c] Therefore digital evidence examination requires forensic analysis of SQLite databases, and the current commercial mobile forensic tools are targeted to performing and presenting this function. However, as alluded to earlier, the ability of tools to reliably perform this function is inconsistent and continuously changing. Reliability is a fundamental principle of forensic science and a requirement for admissibility in court, yet there is an absence in the ability to

[c] The variability of encoding includes fundamental differences in laying down bits (each '1' and '0') in each byte (8 bits). The bytes might be read from left or right or might effectively use 7 of the 8 bits in each byte, with the next bit referring to the next byte. This is an overly simplistic explanation but hopefully provides a sense of the complexity and variability.

objectively compare the relative strengths and weaknesses of different tools due to the lack of a standardised test data set by which the tools can be tested. Digital forensic teams are now able to access a publicly available test data set, a forensic corpus specific to the SQLite database management system, that aims to assist mobile phone forensic tools become more robust, reliable and trustworthy. Critically, digital forensic teams can test the reliability of their suite of tools as used within their own organisation and following their own procedures. The corpus comprises 77 databases grouped into five categories based on their peculiarities, which can then be used to evaluate strengths and weaknesses of existing tools. Importantly the researchers who have put the corpus together and subsequently tested a range of tools and phones note that none of the tested tools handle all of the analyses reliably [14].

The corpus provides a realistic and challenging range of data. The corpus is

- representative of data encountered in the normal course of forensic examinations, including variations in settings, internal structures and contents;
- complex with intertwined information of varying sizes from 2048 bytes to 286,720 bytes;
- presented in human languages with all SQLite encodings represented in the corpus;
- heterogeneously derived from a range of computer systems and usage patterns;
- annotated in order that new algorithms can be validated against earlier versions with extensive documentation regarding the generation of each database;
- available and unrestricted without files that are restricted in any way as all the included data are test data;
- distributed in open file formats with accompanying metadata;
- maintained with versioning and augmented to reflect contemporary and new information that includes major and confounding features of the digital evidence space and mobile forensics in particular;
- inclusive of all SQL statements used to produce the entire corpus;
- inclusive of the SHA256 hash sum of all files to verify the integrity of all databases and their metadata [14].

The corpus includes potential pitfalls, unusual structures and values as can be expected to be encountered in the data of real case work. Each database file includes at least one peculiarity in its contents and/or internal structure. To test the ability of a tool to correctly handle SQL statements, weird table names, encapsulated column definitions and specific SQL keywords and constraints are included. These might include special characters that can be included in column definitions.

There exist three encodings supported by the SQLite file format: UTF-8, UTF16le (little endian) and UTF-16be (big endian) that are used by mobile phone manufacturers. They are, therefore, represented in the corpus with Unicode, Latin and non-Latin (Chinese) characters. The corpus is designed to test the ability of tools to handle different encodings. To test the ability of a tool to handle database elements other than regular tables, some databases include different types of elements, such as virtual and temporary tables.

In normal mobile phone function, when the database contents exceed the length of a page, the record is split and stored on overflow pages. To test the ability of tools to handle tree and page structures, including fragmented contents, different scenarios regarding internal tree and page layouts are included in the corpora. This can include hidden data and pages that do not belong to a database element. As the analysis of deleted data is an important aspect of forensic analysis, particular attention is paid to different settings that can impact deletion actions. To test the ability of a tool to correctly recover deleted contents, databases include deleted and (partially) overwritten data.

The mobile forensic field is now giving considerable attention and is now being given to the exploration of the potential for automated mobile application forensic analysis. One such method is a mobile forensic metamodel that identifies common concepts. The method simplifies the investigation process and enables investigation teams to capture and reuse specialised forensic knowledge that, in turn, supports training and knowledge management. The mobile forensic metamodel clarifies all of the activities conducted in the course of an examination of mobile forensic evidence. Further, as the mobile forensic field includes multiple words and descriptions for similar processes with single words having multiple meanings, the metamodel creates a unified view of the domain and a consistent lexicon. The metamodel defines the relationships between the concepts that form the metamodel into three groupings—*association*, *specialisation* and *aggregation*. *Association* indicates the functional relationship between the concepts, *specialisation* represents the hierarchies between concepts and *aggregation* represents relationships between concepts that are composed of other concepts. The metamodel provides a useful guideline to domain users through the various concepts and who can then find decision solutions from semantic models [15].

Commercial mobile phone forensic vendors use physical acquisition techniques which are appropriate for the full forensic examination of the phone. However, information from mobile phones is often critically important to live investigations necessitating the need for a quick extraction. Some efforts are being made in that direction, for example, an automated differential forensic acquisition technique. The technique and algorithm use baseline data sets and hash comparisons to limit the amount of data acquired from a mobile device. The acquired data are forensically valid bit-for-bit copies of the original data and are obtained in a shortened time, for example, 7 min compared with the usual 1–3 h by traditional methods. Notably the final product is a physical image and is the equivalent of that obtained, albeit sampled, by a traditional method [16].

As mentioned earlier, no single tool extracts all data from a given device. The variability is determined by not only the tool used and the method employed but also the phone make and model, its internal settings, updates etc. By using a combination of tools, a greater net volume of data can be obtained from a given device. If just one tool is to be used, failure to select the correct tool may lead to incomplete and/or improper extraction and, therefore, compromise the integrity of the evidence and diminish its probative value. For example, one tool might be better for recovering text messages, while another might be superior for recovering stand-alone files on a given device. Without the sufficient examiner knowledge and appropriate caveats, the result could be an erroneous analysis, incorrect interpretation and draw wrongful conclusions [17].

A practical way to ensure that the most suitable tool to conduct an examination of a mobile phone and other small devices for a given investigation, especially when time is of the essence and there is only time for one acquisition, a decision-making framework for the selection of the best, most appropriate tool based on the specifics of the case can be established. The decision-making framework can be built on the applied theories of decision analysis: (1) probability theory, noting that, examiners usually select a tool based on previous experience and without actually measuring the performance of the tool, (2) utility theory based on a survey of experts in the field regarding their degree of satisfaction for the relevance of all types of digital evidence and (3) multicriteria decision analysis where the cornerstones of the problem are uncertainties and the utility is associated with different types of digital evidence and the alternative forensic tools.

The framework is based on a multicriteria decision-making process using 19 evaluated criteria that are balanced against performance and relevance as the two main factors. The process has been tested against seven different types of cases, namely, drug trafficking, sexual assault, homicide, credit card fraud, harassment, espionage/eavesdropping and child exploitation and was able to determine a clear difference in performance between two tools for a particular device.

An important application of multimedia forensics that is useful in mobile forensics is to be able to identify the device used for the production of a recorded file. Each recording device has a unique and intrinsic fingerprint that can be used to identify the original of a recording by using the encoding characteristics derived from the MP3 codec identification. Using statistical and mathematical analysis techniques directed to key features of recordings, the method is able to achieve high identification rates of over 97% in the analysis of several makes and models of smartphones. Although it is restricted to the specific formats, MP3, AAC, and M4A, these formats represent the default format of speech recording by most of the popular smartphones [18].

Each brand of phone has distinct and unique features that impact on any forensic analysis that might be conducted. It is useful to consider the unique features of each operating system and of the apps that ae used.

Analysis of android phones

The ability to automate routine processes is the holy grail of digital forensics with many researchers seeking ways to further this aim. One such endeavour is the automated forensic analysis of Android devices using static analysis which can be scaled to a large number of applications without human intervention. It does not require a test environment and can cover all application codes. The model makes use of Android Package (Android APK—the package file format used by the Android operating system for the distribution and installation of mobile apps) to build control flow and data dependency graphs; identify the types of sensitive information written in local storage, then reveals the file path where the information is stored and identifies the structure of the database tables [13]. The system took approximately 64 h and found that approximately one-third of sensitive information that was written to local storage, successfully located the places where sensitive information was written for almost all of the paths and identified the structure of all database tables. Android applications typically have three modes in which information is stored locally: (1) SharedPreferences, (2) database or (3) file. All three modes are accessible to the developed application with a range of data types revealed. It was found that more than half of the Android applications leak sensitive information and more than one-third write sensitive information to local storage making Android phones especially useful in digital investigations.

Mobile apps are becoming increasingly popular as the preferred mode of communication. Therefore, an alternative approach to consider when conducting a digital forensic investigation might be to extract and examine specific mobile applications, rather than the whole device. This approach can apply in situations where the digital evidence pertaining to one or more specific applications is acquired from the device. An automated forensic analysis can be scaled to a large number of applications so that no human intervention is required. Such an approach would be especially useful where an investigation involved, for example, numerous coconspirators who were communicating using apps. Such an approach has been developed and tested on 100 applications where 36 applications were found to have written information to local storage. Further, noting that Android applications typically have three storage modes—SharedPreferences, database or file—the application was able to handle all three modes and to identify the structure of the databases where the information was stored [13].

In demonstrating the differences between tools and the importance of physical acquisitions versus logical acquisitions in mobile forensic analysis, experiments were conducted using a Samsung mobile phone with a 16 GB internal memory and 1 GB RAM which was seeded with data of a variety of sources. The phone was then factory reset to simulate deletion of the preloaded data and as a person might do if engaging in illegal activity or work of a secure nature and wished to remove all evidence. The phone was then imaged and examined using a range of common commercial mobile forensic tools. Analysis of the logical acquisitions did not reveal any data files. Analysis of physical acquisitions revealed less than 100% of the phone memory when acquired by multiple tools. Images obtained using different acquisition tools yielded differences in the volume of the evidence recovered when analysed and there were significant differences in the yields of various file types. No one tool performed best for all file types and most of the tested tools recovered major file formats that other tools did not recover, therefore, reaffirming that no single forensic tool recovers all evidence on a phone [11].

With many phone manufacturers using Android operating systems, there are many Android applications on the market with a count of 2.9 million as of March 2020 [19]. Associated with this growth, which has increased the attack surface for Android devices, there has been an increase in security threats attributed to Android applications. An Android application is a single file in the Android application package (APK) format which might comprise (1) a file containing essential data about the application which the phone must read before it can run the code and (2) at least one Android Virtual Machine Dalvik Executable (DEX) file which is the application itself. An alternative approach for analysing 11,711 Android apps researchers were able to rapidly query data directly from the DEX binary files and demonstrate a markedly improved efficiency in comparison with other existing tools reducing the total query time (for 11,695 applications tested) from 1368 min to 88 min [20].

Huawei smartphones

The growing presence of Huawei smartphones in the consumer market means that the ability to examine Huawei phones is becoming increasingly important. Generally, smartphones are usually backed up locally on the device's internal storage and on a PC. However, some of the backup data is encrypted to protect privacy, which the forensic examiner must decrypt before it can be analysed. If the backup data has been encrypted with a user-controlled value, such as a password or personal identification number (PIN), recovering that value should take priority [21].

The smartphone backup application and its PC backup programme can be reverse engineered to reveal the local and PC backup processes, including the password-based encryption. Local backup is performed by the phone itself and the data are stored in the internal memory, an SD card or a USB drive. The local backup requires a password and the encryption only applies to database files. The PC backup is synchronised between the phone and the PC via a USB connection. Unlike the local backup the PC encrypts both database and media files and will do so even in the absence of a password.

It is believed to be impossible to decrypt password-based encrypted data on Huawei smartphones without a user-entered password. Therefore, to decrypt the data, it is necessary to recover the password of which there are four password recovery methods, that is, four different password authenticators. Two of the password recovery authenticators are created during the backup process. The third password authenticator is in a 'backupinfo.ini' file created after backup on the PC. The fourth method is a plain text attack media file based on the user-entered password. Each password recovery method takes time with estimates ranging from less than a minute to multiple years.

Apps

The popularity and utility of apps continue to grow with an estimated 204 billion mobile downloaded apps worldwide in 2019 and over 258 billion downloads of apps by 2022 [22]. Instant messaging via apps has become an essential means of communication exceeding that of voice calls and SMS. Instant messaging applications have pervaded beyond personal use and are now increasingly used for business and professional communications. But apps are also used to facilitate criminal activities.

LINE

LINE has increased in popularity as a communications app growing from 170 million users from the second quarter of 2014 to 217 million users by the fourth quarter of 2016 and is particularly popular in Asia where it is ranked as the second most popular instant messaging app. LINE uses unencrypted messages. Underscoring the point that different tools will acquire differing artefacts, two tools, Oxygen and MOBILedit, were used to examine digital evidence from the LINE messenger app. Oxygen was able to acquire LINE text message artefacts using physical acquisition and to perform timeline analysis for calls, messages, calendar events, geolocation data and application activities, whereas MOBILedit was able to obtain contact information, text messages, deleted data and pictures, but video artefacts could not be obtained. The picture artefacts include metadata such as file path, file size and dates created and modified [23].

BlackBerry messenger

BlackBerry Messenger is one of the world's most popular smartphone instant messaging apps that enjoys a high uptake in Britain, India, South Africa and Indonesia. It was originally designed only for smartphones using the BlackBerry operating system but is now available on Android, iOS and Windows platforms. The use of the tool *Andrilla* on a Sony Xperia Z running Android Lollipop was able to acquire several messages that enabled the reconstruction of the conversation, but images could not be displayed. Reports and logs could be generated in HTML format and text files and contained email accounts, Wi-Fi passwords, applications, SMS and call logs. The text file report included the date of data acquisition, Android version, IMEI and other data [24].

iPhone health app

The iPhone health app automatically collects activity data for health purposes, including the number of steps taken and distance travelled, which are recorded with timestamps. In addition to the Health app that is shipped with the iPhone, users can access other apps and wearable sensors that can be synced with the Health app where the data, or a copy, can be stored. The information could be very useful in forensic investigation in a number of scenarios including, but not limited to, assessing probability statements, in the form of a likelihood ratio, about scenarios or routes or the analysis of physical user activity over time. It is important to note that the reliability of Health app information cannot be assumed [25].

In a study of five subjects using iPhone 6, iPhone 7 and iPhone 8, the accuracy of steps and distances was assessed under a range of conditions and against manual measurements. Variables that were tested included carrying locations such as in trouser pockets, jacket pockets, backpack and hand; walking and running and a range of distances travelled. The data for the number of steps taken were found to correlate well the manual measurements, apart from a few outliers. The distances registered by the iPhones were found to be dependent on the carrying location, the walking speed and the walking style of the subjects. For example, a walking (or running) style with vigorous arm movements led to higher registered distances travelled. Although little information is available as to how the app functions, it was determined that the geolocation APIs are not utilised by the Health app during locomotion, which means that it is reliant on accelerometer and gyroscope sensor data.

Snapchat

Snapchat is a popular social network app that is available for Android and iOS devices. It allows users to send messages, photos and videos with a predetermined time to view. Once the time has expired, the contents are automatically deleted and are no longer available to view by the recipient. An examination for potential Snapchat artefacts on an Android platform was conducted using two forensic tools—Autopsy and AXIOM

Examine [26]. Autopsy was able to view ~10% of Snapchat images and videos and some basic information. But it was not able to indicate deleted snaps, chat messages, user information and friends. AXIOM Examine presented event logs, sent snaps, 100% of friends, 100% user information, 58% of chat messages and 6% of delivered video with detailed information such as sender, receiver, time and status. But AXIOM was not able to indicate deleted information, story, and delivered photo snaps. Using both tools manually, more artefacts could be found.

Kik

Kik is a relatively new messaging app that has quickly grown popular among young people with 300 million users. The marketing appeal was the promise of anonymity as users were not required to provide personal details, a phone number, verify an email address or, importantly, verify the individual's age. Consequently, verifying the identity of the Kik user can be difficult for the forensic examiner. The app has gained a reputation as a preferred app for child abusers and those engaging in cyber bullying. Although the owner company was on the verge of closing down the app due to a dispute with regulators, it was acquired by a holding company, MediaLab, which will invest in its future. Kik do not store data on its servers; therefore they cannot retrieve any sent or received messages. The only means of retrieving any forensic evidence is via a forensic examination of the device and, possibly, the backup [27, 28].

Ovens and Morison [28] studied forensic artefacts produced by the use of Kik on iOS devices. When iTunes was used to perform a logical acquisition (not primary purpose of the iTunes program) of the target device, message attachments and Kik-related files on the iOS device with names and suffixes suggestive of their content were found. However, the filenames are obscure. Contact information and also other Kik users suggested by the search engine when the *Find People* feature is used can be retrieved, in addition to bots run by Kik's administrators and marketing companies. Additional information is also available that suggests the frequency of communication between the user and the group in group chats.

Messages from blocked users are delivered to the device but are invisible to the user, unless the user unblocks the corresponding party. Message data include message content, sender/receiver information, timestamps and chronology. Also the data indicated if the messages were direct between two users or part of a group chat. The date and time of blocking and unblocking was not apparent. Deleted contacts and chats could be recovered by the examiner in the kik.sqlite database and entire conversations could be retrieved even when the conversation had been deleted.

When a Kik user sends a video or image, it is uploaded to the Kik servers and a copy is stored on the device along with a preview version of the attachment. The recipient is notified of a new message if permitted. On opening the Kik app, all chats are automatically updated and the attachments downloaded. Attachments can also be retrieved from the Kik servers via a web browser using the URL that can be found on the device. Attachments that have been deleted from the Kik app can still be retrieved from the iOS device and the Kik server for 8 weeks and 4 weeks, respectively. Moreover, preview versions are still recoverable from the device and backed up on iTunes for 3 months after deletion.

WeChat

WeChat is one of the world's most popular instant messaging smartphone and social media apps. The app has multimedia capabilities including text, images, voice and video, in addition to services such as WeChat Moments (where users share their lives with friends) and Official Accounts. To protect the privacy of users, WeChat encrypts the database of messages and data acquisition through the backup functionality is prohibited. By the end of 2015, there were 697 million active users in over 200 countries and is the instant messaging mobile application with the highest number of Chinese users. The app is used widely by criminals for communication and for the organisation and coordination of criminal acts such as selling illegal items, fraud and child exploitation. The ability to retrieve and interpret data from WeChat is, therefore, an essential source of evidence for investigation [29].

In a study of multiple versions of WeChat (version 5.0 through to version 6.3.27) on six different Android smartphones, one of the successful solutions involved downgrading the WeChat version to version 6.0 as later versions cannot back up the data using the backup command. The SQLite database of the user's chat messages is encrypted, although the decryption key can be calculated from data stored on the phone, that is, the identity of the phone itself and user-specific information. The specific retrieval details of all the various types of messages are quite varied as the different types (text, images, audio and video) have different storage schemes, for example, 'Moments' are stored unencrypted. The multimedia resources can be acquired from the WeChat server after extracting the URL of the multimedia file and the thumbnails can also be extracted from the device.

Telegram

Telegram is a cloud-based instant messaging and voice-over IP service. It is available for Android, iOS, Windows Phone,[d] Windows NT, macOS and Linux. As of March 2018, Telegram had 200 million active users. Messages are encrypted by default on the server, and client–server communication is encrypted. Telegram accounts are tied to phone numbers and verified by SMS. There has been little published research regarding the analysis of Telegram messages.

WhatsApp

WhatsApp is a smartphone communication app owned by Facebook. As of February 2020, WhatsApp has over 2 billion users in over 180 countries, is the world's most popular messaging app and is the primary means of communication in many countries. It can be used on several platforms including Android, BlackBerry, iOS and Symbian and can be used for secure calls, text, video, images and audio messages. Registration requires a mobile phone number. Importantly, WhatsApp uses end-to-end encryption on all platforms. One approach to forensic analysis of the WhatsApp content is to use text mining to process the evidence. The text mining process employs word weighting to obtain a value comparison of a conversation between two actors and cosine similarity to calculate the similarity between two objects [30].

[d] Windows phone is now discontinued.

Skype, Viber and WhatsApp on android

The three most popular mobile voice-over Internet protocol (mVoIP) apps available from the Google Play (Android) store are Skype, Viber and WhatsApp messenger. Experiments were conducted using both logical and physical extractions from an Android device with a rootkit installed and examined using a range of tools—Access Data FTK Imager, SQLite Database browser, Internet Evidence Finder and Epoch & Unix Timestamp Converter.[e]

For WhatsApp Messenger, unique directories could be found that include information records and logs related to the sent and received activities of the user: contacts and chat messages, pictures, audio and video. For Viber, two unique directories were found and included contact information, calls made and received and GPS coordinates. Similarly, comprehensive information was found for the Skype experiments, in addition to the IP address of the device which provides further information concerning the location of the user [31].

Clocks

One of the questions that is often asked of the digital forensic examiner will concern that of timelines, i.e. what is the chronology of events and at what time did events occur. It is standard procedure for the examiner to document the clock settings for court and often assumed that any changes to the clock are not automatic but are due to a deliberate intervention by the owner of the device or another person. Using the app on a phone to document the time is not a forensically sound method to determine the time of a data event and should not be presented as evidence in judicial proceedings.

The reliability of clocks on battery-powered devices is assumed to be high and that clocks are accurate. This is despite the well-known phenomenon that different tools will display different dates and times for the same events on the same device, for example, when different time and date conventions are used if different countries. Physical clocks can be affected by the environmental and other conditions to which it has been subjected and can result in a loss of accuracy over time. The precision or otherwise of the information contained within the files and logs can be undetermined which may lead to uncertainty in interpretation of the evidence. The multiple sources of potential error can include the uncertainty of the source of information, incorrect logs, information loss and other errors. If the possibility of error exists, then it is important that the examiner performing the examination have accounted for the potential sources of error and the associated uncertainties.

One such condition is a failing battery that will supply a reduced current to the clock. The battery will power the phone until the lower limit for normal operations is reached at which point it will shut the device down but will retain enough power to maintain the clock. If additional power is not provided to the device, the phone will completely shut down including the clock.

[e] A rootkit allows privileged access to the device's Android operating system and can be used in forensic examination of Android devices.

Timestamps are a crucial part the evidence in digital forensic analysis and interpretation. For example, when data carving techniques are used to examine only that data concerning events occurring at specific time intervals, an incorrect timestamp could lead to the inclusion of information concerning events that occurred at some other time. Conversely, relevant information with an incorrect timestamp and erroneously indicating that it occurred outside of the period of time under investigation could be excluded. Another example might be when patterns of behaviour, such as a daily routine, are being documented and an incorrect clock will mislead the determination of the behavioural patterns.

The examiner can use a hypothesis-based approach to determine whether or not a clock has been adjusted. The timestamps are then used to test the clock hypothesis by looking at causally linked events and timestamps outside of the possible set of timestamps for a particular clock. A processor can have multiple clock sources and uses the power-saving clock when the processor is in its sleep state. The power-saving clock is the less precise clock. During normal processor operations, the more precise and power-consuming clock is used.

Once the decision that a phone should be subjected to a forensic examination, it should be isolated from the Internet to reduce the possibility of the clock being corrected had it been previously altered in some way.

The same principle also applies to Internet of Things devices. The growing number of such devices will, therefore, lead to digital forensics examiners encountering a growing number of devices with failing or low-powered batteries, operating outside the prescribed operating temperature or in some other less than ideal environment. It is thought that IoT devices are more likely to be impacted by low-voltage states impacting the accuracy of the clock as many such devices are smaller and designed for reduced power consumption.

Network forensics

Network forensics is similar to device forensics, except that it deals with dynamic, transient and volatile data instead of static and stored data, i.e. the crime scene is constantly changing. Network forensics is the scientific process that ensures the investigation of attacks that are performed in a network or network devices. Current network forensic processes do not address the forensic challenges presented by new networks such as Internet of Things. Network forensics is in need of considerable research effort in order to meet the challenges of IoT and 5G [32]. Meanwhile, digital and network forensic examiners are largely flying blind in their need to apply and translate existing knowledge to a dynamic and volatile environment.

The validity and integrity of data can be compromised by failures in system security, of which intrusion detection systems are an integral part. Intrusion detection systems generally include a sniffing process, observing data traffic and traffic log analysis. SQL injection is a technique used to exploit web applications that store data in a database. An attacker can take advantage of SQL syntax and capabilities by influencing what is forwarded to the database. Detection of SQL injection attacks is identified by a range of forensic evidence that is collected, checked, analysed and reported on. The evidence can be collected from various sources depending on the given situation and can include the web server, network switch, router, cloud, email and the suspect's source device. Using forensic tools on the web server can provide information concerning SQL injection attacks and identify unauthorised actions that have occurred. With the rapidly growing number of IoT devices attached to the Internet, a greater attack surface comprising multiple vulnerabilities is presented to would-be attackers. The range of vulnerabilities can include attacks on the physical device (microprobing and reverse engineering), side channels (timing, power and electromagnetic), environmental, crypto (ciphertext, known plain, chosen plain and man in the middle); software (virus, Trojan, logic bomb, worms and denial of service) and network (monitor and eavesdropping, traffic, camouflage, denial of service, node subversion or malfunction or capture or outage, message comption, false node, replication and routing). Clearly, the range of vulnerabilities is large and there is much to be considered in any investigation. Researchers are developing models to analyse the large volumes of data that are produced in an attack [33].

Internet of Things

The Internet of Things (IoT) is a global distributed network connecting physical objects that are capable of sensing or acting on their environment and are able to communicate with each other, other machines or computers. These objects can include simple items with embedded sensors such as household appliances including refrigerators, industrial robots, cars, trains, wearable technology, early warning tide measuring buoys and air-monitoring balloons [10, 34]. IoT can also include the management and control of buildings, such as the heating and cooling systems, lighting and security systems, or for traffic control in cities. The impetus for the growth of the IoT is driven by business need to provide better, more efficient services and the provision of societal benefits. The data generated by IoT systems, once generated, can then be accessed via web-based applications to interpret and represent the data to users and decision-makers, such as healthcare professionals and meteorologists for action.

Analysis of the IoT-collected data produces insights and identifies opportunities for improvements including cost efficiencies and safety. It is estimated that the IoT will comprise 25 billion connected objects by the end of 2020 with the rapid growth assisted by the rapidly falling price of sensor and radio-frequency identification (RFID) technology and the greater coverage and availability of wireless and mobile networks. In addition, Internet Protocol version 6 supports sufficient IP addresses for 3.4×10^{38} Internet-connected devices. This presents a challenge to law enforcement investigations as it can allow for the rapid and frequent change of IP addresses for example, to obscure nefarious activities. Identifying the IP address of a device involved in criminal activity, whether it is as the suspect, victim or witness, is often a key piece of information in the investigation process.

Internet of Things devices communicate with each other directly or via application programming interfaces (API) over the Internet and they can be controlled by learned devices with high computing capabilities. The growth in the prevalence of IoT devices now presents a much great attack surface for interference including viruses, mass surveillance, denial of service and disruption of IoT networks. Digital forensics is a key capability in the investigation of these attacks. Notably, however, current digital forensic tools and standard procedures, as the digital forensics community currently understands them, are not ideal for investigations of IoT devices. For example, IoT devices generate large volumes of diverse data in formats that can be confusing to digital forensic practitioners and the lack of real-time log analysis solutions does not help. Notably, the key evidence that is physically present on the devices must be extracted from the firmware or flash memory which is not necessarily a routine forensic procedure for forensic examiners. In addition, the data from IoT systems are usually stored and processed in the cloud therefore presenting access issues for the investigators. This is exacerbated by the two-tier (the device and the cloud) processing and storage of data, where computation is mostly performed at the edge of the network (the device) and metadata is stored in the cloud. Finally, the proprietary nature of hardware and software that reflects the vendor's specific design and infrastructure philosophy and used in IoT devices will generate bespoke encoding of the digital traces [35].

One potential solution to these challenges is to broadly group IoT devices with a view to constructing an IoT digital forensic taxonomy. By grouping into smart home, smart vehicles, smartphones, drones, BitTorrent Sync peer-to-peer cloud storage service and general IoT systems, it is much easier to develop and disentangle the multitude of IoT systems. The taxonomy can then be further broken down into (1) forensic phases, (2) enablers, (3) networks, (4) sources of evidence, (5) investigation modes, (6) forensic models, (7) forensic layers, (8) forensic tools and (9) forensic data processing. There are, however, further issues to be addressed to effectively and efficiently conduct IoT forensic examinations, including (1) managing the IoT data volume in a structure that can store and manage the diverse types of data that has been generated by various IoT devices; (2) mitigation of privacy risks; (3) data integration across the spectrum of all data sources including IoT, social media and other communications generated data and (4) dealing with system identification and human behaviours to form a predictive model to locate relevant evidence.

IoT devices pose a number of security risks to consumers and businesses including access to sensitive data through the unauthorised access to devices or the interception of communications or access to servers or cloud services that aggregate the large amounts of IoT data. Hackers could take control of systems or networks to cause disruption as an act of mischief or for ransom and might include a power grid, a personal health device or a motor vehicle. A high proportion of devices themselves will lack the power and physical size to provide the acceptable level of security which leaves the data more vulnerable [36].

As the IoT comprises the broad categories of cloud, virtualisation, mobile devices, fixed computing, sensor and RFID technologies and artificial intelligence, forensic examination will require analysis of devices and data in all of these categories. Consequently, digital forensic processes that are applied to large data investigations can be expected to be applied to investigations involving the IoT. As the IoT further evolves and develops, additional devices, including new and unfamiliar special purpose devices that capture, process and transmit data, will contribute data that is of probative value to investigations [37, 38].

Conventional digital forensic processes recommend that devices should not be turned off if they are running when encountered by first responders in order to preserve file metadata [39, 40]. As the standards that have applied to digital evidence investigations in the emerging cloud computing environment have changed, the same holds true with the greater complexity encountered in IoT investigations. For example, devices that are left running at the crime scene will consume power and may overwrite stored data due to restricted storage capacities. Consideration needs to be given to whether the power should be switched off or to leave the device and system running.

The data from IoT devices can be in many, often proprietary, formats that can impact on digital forensic processes. The proprietary formats, protocols and physical interfaces all add further challenge to IoT investigations and complicate the extraction of evidence. Some systems distribute data to adjacent nodes or to cloud services to varying degrees. Therefore a comprehensive investigation plan might require access to data from other nodes, base stations or cloud services. When the data from multiple devices is merged and combined with data from other sources, then considered together with other information concerning the circumstances of an investigation, investigators are provided with a rich context of information concerning the chronology of events that have taken place in the physical world. IoT is an ambient intelligence in which the environment is reacting to the user's requirements without any conscious interaction by the user. In fact, criminals likely will be oblivious to the incriminating information that can be recorded on IoT systems. One of the major challenges with digital forensics is to be able to 'place the person at the keyboard'. Biometric information and personal identity are often built into IoT devices, so the information and logs from the devices can, therefore, lead to the identification of a person of interest. In addition, smart homes with security systems often have biometric data stored within the cloud.

As can be seen from the above, analysis of digital traces on IoT devices is not a simple process. Most smart homes lack any forensic preparedness and therefore they are not well placed to become the scene of a crime from which good forensic evidence can be obtained. Smart home devices, comprising elements such as multifunctional surveillance cameras, an alarm system with a base station, motion sensors, contact sensors, a smoke detector and a CO detector, might produce digital traces that can be extracted from the devices themselves and the associated smartphone applications. Traces generated by the devices can be found not only on the physical devices themselves but also on the smartphones and in the cloud. Traces from the devices could provide information such as when a door was opened or when an alarm was disabled, whereas the digital traces that were available on the smartphone might include cached image thumbnails and fragments of camera streams, cached events triggered by the sensors and event logs. The traces provide investigators with information concerning what happened, including which user account sent commands to the device and recorded images and video. In addition, cloud account credentials might also be recovered from the smartphone applications. It is not straightforward though and, due to the technical complexity alluded to earlier, there are many confounding factors. For example, an increasing amount of network traffic is encrypted, and communication protocols between the device and the base station are not limited to Wi-Fi and Ethernet; some devices use ZigBee, Z-Wave, Bluetooth or custom radio frequencies. The traces on the devices themselves might be limited to configuration settings, or might be present only for a limited period of time due to limited memory or until a reboot, or could only be accessed by nonautomated techniques such as JTAG or chip off [41].

When considering the four phases of the digital forensic investigation process (identification, preservation, analysis and presentation) for IoT devices [42], each phase must be considered within the paradigm of IoT.

When performing the search and seizure of the evidence, it is not always immediately apparent where the evidential data are being stored or where it came from. If it is stored in a cloud system that happens to be in another jurisdiction and/or subject to differing privacy and security regulations, gaining access to the data can become more difficult.

One potential solution is the integration of IoT device data into building information modelling which is a digital representation of the physical and functional characteristics of a facility. This process can assist in answering the questions of the source, location, format and encoding of the information. It would assist in reducing the data set from which the examiner is trying to identify the probative evidence and designate the nature of the data.

When considering the preservation of evidence, the complexity is greater in IoT than it is in terrestrial forensics or cloud forensics. Improvements to the security of operating systems began when malware writers began reducing the evidence of their presence on the victim's hard drive and started exploiting the random-access memory (RAM) for the storage of information. Extracting process memory from RAM was more difficult than for hard drive evidence, so forensic examiners began developing methods for recovering process memory [43].

Once the evidence has been identified, there remains a serious challenge to its preservation. It is possible, or even probable, that the data of interest will be overwritten and/or compressed if the devices are unable to interact with the cloud to store their data and the amount of data generated exceeds the storage capacity of the device itself.[f] The data must be reliable and trustworthy to be of probative value, therefore its origin must be demonstrated beyond a reasonable doubt. Aggregation of the data and loss due to compression may alter the data to such a degree that it is difficult to demonstrate a linear link between the data and its context. The lack of a demonstrable link can cause serious challenges to the presentation of evidence.

The volume of data comprising the IoT domain has doubled every 2 years between 2012 and 2020 to reach an estimate of 40,000 exabytes, having risen from a base of 130 exabytes in 2005 [44]. The consequence of such growth means that the time and resources that spent finding relevant, probative evidence in this greater volume and then putting it into a form that can be analysed will be challenging. Digital forensic investigators will require new skills to efficiently and effectively collect all relevant evidence from the various devices that has potentially travelled through different networks leaving behind a digital trail concerning a particular incident or investigation [45]. Furthermore, IoT devices can be potentially unreliable as the data can be changed

[f] http://www.ijcaonline.org/research/volume139/number10/yakubu-2016-ijca-909390.pdf.

without human input and before it is acquired by investigators as the devices learn and adjust to their environment based on sensory input [39].

In order to conduct forensic investigations involving IoT devices, established digital forensic knowledge, methods and techniques will need to be built upon in recognition that IoT forensics is different to terrestrial forensics and even cloud forensics. Methods and tools will need to be developed and employed that assure the acquisition of all relevant evidence in a time efficient manner. At the same time, the evidence must be forensically sound so that it can be exhibited in a manner that provides the court with sufficient comfort in its veracity. The collection procedures must also account for the need that the evidence will most likely be obtained in parallel to the incident response in all affected networks and devices without modification of the evidence.

By definition and design, smart homes and other IoT environments are connected and dynamic and can be altered from anywhere and at anytime. Many IoT devices have sensors or actuators that generate data, sometimes autonomously and sometimes in response to human actions and other environmental stimuli. This always ‘on and active’ mode makes them excellent digital witnesses that constantly generate and record digital traces that can potentially be used in investigations.

The great number and variety of devices, the heterogeneity of protocols and their distributed nature present a huge trove of data that can be exploited by the examiner, as long as the examiner can manage the totality of the data generated. The forensic examination of Internet of Things devices, however, is not supported by existing digital forensic tools and methods, making it difficult to extract and interpret data from them without the support from an advisor with specialised knowledge in that area.

Several studies of digital traces on IoT smartphone applications have been undertaken. For example, the digital traces that were obtainable on devices and systems such as Arlo, Askey, Echo, iSmartAlarm, Netgear, Nest, QBee and Wink have been compared with Amazon Echo and Nest camera [46]. There is such a plethora of devices and systems that not all can be documented as each generates, processes and stores data in its own propriety way. The types of data that can be obtained include movement, location, temperature, presence/absence, steps taken, distance walked, time spent walking and calories burnt. As many IoT systems are managed through an app on a smartphone, the digital traces in the smartphone app might include cached thumbnail images and fragments of camera streams, cached events triggered by the sensors, complete event logs stored in the application database; and cloud account credentials which can be used to obtain data, including data unrelated to the IoT system, that might be stored on the cloud system. The digital traces can provide information about what happened, when and which user account sent commands to the device. Image thumbnails can potentially provide information regarding the number of people in an IoT environment and their identities. Photographs and videos could potentially provide information concerning the physical attributes of specific individuals. Each device and system presents a new challenge for examination and an individualised examination method will be required.

IoT devices, especially for smart homes, are typically monitored and managed through an app on a smartphone. The app will store information about the device, its configuration and past events. Forensic investigation of the app, however, will require manual investigation as mobile forensic software usually does not parse IoT device data. In a test environment, in-depth manual analysis of the smartphone app, including reverse engineering, can uncover additional information that can be correlated to corresponding events recorded by the device itself. The in-depth analysis can be codified by writing custom plugins for digital forensic tools to automatically process the traces.

It is important for the examiner to analyse the vulnerabilities of IoT devices so that potential compromise and exploitation of a device by a malicious actor can be understood. In addition, vulnerability analysis will assist in discovering methods for acquiring data from the device.

It might be possible to conduct a physical analysis of the device using a serial connection (UART) and/or JTAG or by using chip-off techniques to directly access the device memory. Most network traffic associated with IoT devices is encrypted which further complicates a forensic examination, although some devices communicate in plain text.

Cardiac implantable medical devices, such as defibrillators and pacemakers, are increasingly being used to treat patients in the management of health conditions. The devices are surgically implanted and wirelessly configured by healthcare professionals. Generally the wireless communication to the device is insecure rendering the devices vulnerable to attack. Consequently a forensic analysis of the digital traces might be pertinent as a part of the postmortem examination if a lethal attack on the device is suspected. The postmortem analysis would seek to establish (1) what functions of the implanted device were impacted, i.e. either did not execute its action or executed it incorrectly; (2) the role of the malfunctioning of the device in the health event; (3) the malfunctioning was due malicious intent or improper deployment; (4) the attack scenario and (5) the vulnerabilities that were exploited [47].

Interpretation of digital traces obtained from implanted devices is unique to that of other sources of digital evidence as the (1) consequences of an action of an implanted device will vary from one patient to the next, (2) implanted devices are resource constrained and (3) the evidence is technical and medical, and therefore, it should be interpreted by a multidisciplinary team comprising a range of experts. The postmortem examination of the digital traces is a three-step process that identifies the cause of death, reconstruction of the scenario that would result in those specific traces and correlation of the technical and medical data.

Access to the memory/file system can be accessed on some devices, and therefore the memory dump can be acquired and may provide useful data, for example, the password for the private Wi-Fi network, a partial file system copy of the device, the cameras that were connected to the station and their last settings, the logs from the device's last factory reset such as time stamps, or the motion detector events from the connected camera.

There are many challenges posed by digital traces that are collected from IoT devices and the managing smartphone apps, including the quantity of data with much of it being unstructured or not explicit. Parsers can be developed to automate the extraction of the traces in a structured and understandable form, for example, to extract cloud credentials, events, user action and debug logs and to parse interesting events.

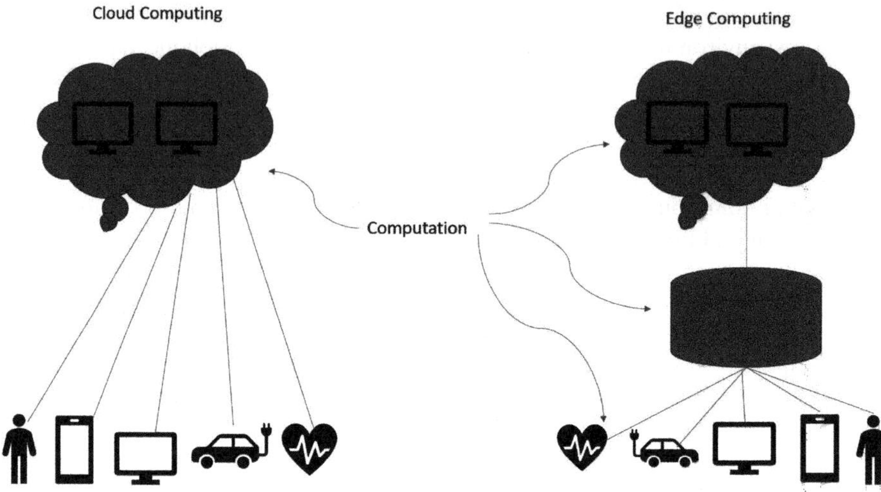

Fig. 13.1 Cloud vs. image edge computing.

When a digital evidence examiner encounters a new IoT device, the first step of the investigation is to survey existing research on the device. The research materials might include academic research, security sources such as vulnerability databases and other community resources. The research will reveal information about traces and vulnerabilities that are already known for the device and ways in which to gain root access to the device which will enable the device to be directed to give up its evidence.

IoT forensics presents additional challenges beyond the technical ones. Traditional digital forensics has generally not required the voluntary participation of citizens and relatively little regard has been paid to privacy. IoT devices, however, function more as a digital witness for which voluntary participation of citizens is required and can only be achieved if the privacy of individuals is guaranteed [48] (Fig. 13.1).

Drones

Drones, or unmanned aerial vehicles, have grown in popularity among hobbyists and for commercial use alike. They are also being used in law enforcement for surveillance, in farming for agricultural maintenance, monitoring of poaching of wild life in Africa and for acquiring specialist movie and sports event footage. There are also reports of the technology being used for nefarious purposes such as physical assaults; intrusions into protected places such as the UK Parliament, the Royal residences, the White House, prisons and to interfere with civil aviation. Given the increased popularity of drones, including the use for nefarious purposes, there is an increasing requirement for the forensic analysis of these devices.

Each drone manufacturer has there own design philosophy and architecture. The generation of data by the drone device, its subsequent processing and storage will vary greatly between manufacturers and also between the models that each manufacturer offers. During the course of a digital forensic examination of a drone, the examiner will encounter four challenges that will need to be addressed: (1) Acquiring the data can be difficult as gaining direct access the physical disk for imaging can be complex; (2) establishing the location and flight path (central to the establishment of any offences) from the data recording will differ between manufacturers, may not be recorded at all by the device but recorded only on the controller; (3) metadata of media stored by the device might provide geolocation data and (4) establishing ownership of the drone can be difficult if the device has been abandoned. These challenges can be made even more difficult with the growing availability of components from an international supply chain enabling to build their own vehicles and specify their own customisations. Some researchers have been devoting time and energy to the acquisition and analysis of drones, including the device's internal storage, interpretation of in-flight data, captured media and the operating system. Since drones can be also controlled via Android (for example Samsung) and iOS (Apple) mobile devices, analysis of the digital traces from these devices is also recommended and used to corroborate, complement and supplement those traces obtained from the drone device provided that the owner can be identified and the mobile devices obtained [49].

Establishing ownership and control of a drone device can be problematic due to the ability to operate and command remotely and at some distance from the crime scene. A drone owner might be quite willing to sacrifice the drone device and abandon it at the crime scene or take steps for it to self-destruct. Artificial intelligence can be also used to control and direct drone devices therefore further distancing and obscuring the ownership and control of the device. A sound forensic investigation of a drone will include consideration of all forensic evidence including DNA and fingerprints which might assist in establishing ownership of the device and provide a line of investigation in order to, among other benefits, identify additional sources of evidence. Once the drone device has been secured, it should be powered down to prevent the data being compromised. As drones continue to grow in popularity, it can be reasonably expected that their use for illegal activities will also increase, as will the range of drone manufacturers and models in the market. Consequently, examination of the range of drones that become associated with criminal activity is likely to present and be analogous to, the challenges faced in mobile forensics, i.e. a growing range of devices and operating systems that examiners will expect to encounter. Other methods of data acquisition, including JTAG and chip off, are also likely to be appropriate for the analysis of drones.

New devices and apps

There has been much discussion in the media and within the forensic science and the cyber security communities of the Internet of Things. Perhaps the most pervasive of these devices are the digital virtual assistants[g] such as Amazon Alexa, Google Assistant and Apple's Siri, but similar devices from other vendors are also appearing

[g] The term 'digital virtual assistants' has been used for consistency in this review. As it is a new field, there are alternative naming conventions employed by some authors.

on the market. All three of the main offerings feature voice matching technology, 'delete recording' options and instant translation technology; are compatible with a range of Internet of Things brands and support multiple languages. As can be imagined, as each device is in 'always on' mode, they will be rich in the data that has been captured and will present challenges for digital forensic examiners to retrieve and interpret the digital traces [50].

Digital virtual assistants are designed to act in an ecosystem where they can access cloud services (such as Alexa cloud services and other clouds), use companion devices (personal computers, mobile devices and smart devices), access third-party applications (for example pizza delivery and ride sharing) and communicate with other IoT devices (including smart lighting and smart smoke alarms among others). The Amazon Echo family of devices, including the Dot and Tap, connect to the intelligent cloud-based voice service known as Alexa. The digital mesh is becoming further established with emerging convergence of Alexa with connected cars, smart refrigerators and robots [51, 52].

The new IoT technologies demand a new forensic approach, one that combines cloud-side and client-side forensics. To demonstrate, we can consider the example of the Alexa range of devices and their supporting ecosystem. The device operations are executed on the virtual digital assistant device which sends the digital artefacts to the cloud where they reside. To access these artefacts, valid user accounts are required, but it is difficult to recover deleted data from the cloud. A multilevel forensic strategy is required that analyses the digital traces from the hardware (the device), the network to understand the communications between each component and the client(s) (the mobile apps and web browsers on the users smartphone) which are used to set up and manage Alexa-enabled devices and the cloud.

In addition to the well-known AI virtual digital assistant offerings from Google, Samsung, Apple and Amazon, more recent offerings are now available from large and international companies including *Xiaomi* and *Alibaba* (Chinese) and *Clova* of Naver, *Kajao I* of KAKAO, *NUGU* of SKT and *GiGA Genie* of KT (Republic of Korea).

Despite their recent appearance in the consumer market, digital evidence obtained from digital virtual assistants have already been used in several homicide investigations. Consistent with taking a multilayered approach, it is recommended that comprehensive approaches are used to acquire and analyse digital traces, both to ensure that all available digital evidence is obtained and to validate the results observed between the elements of the ecosystem. There are five analysis techniques that can be applied to the ecosystem:

1. Packet analysis via the AI speaker examines the communication process between the AI speaker and the cloud as the data packets are collected in real time.
2. Packet analysis via the smartphone app examines the communication between the application and the cloud as the user information data are collected in real time.
3. Directory analysis of the data that is stored by the smartphone app. The smartphone app communicates with the cloud while using applications such as AI speaker configuration and voice commands. Artefacts available in the app include personal information, connected speaker information and voice command information.
4. For Android smartphones, Android Application Package (APK) decompilation analysis looks at the communication between an Android mobile app with the cloud to process the

user's voice input. These data can reveal the API address and the data transmitted to the server and other data stored on the server of the device. The equivalent analytical processes can be applied to other, non-Android smartphones.

5. AI speaker chip-off analysis studies user the identity information of the device required for the cloud to recognise the user, the user's personal information and device history information. The information can include, for example, the user's name and address.

The forensic strategy for a given device and ecosystem will depend on the way in which the vendor has designed the ecosystem and how it has been configured on installation. For example, in situations where no smartphone apps are linked to the assistant, some of the methods cannot be used. Some assistants reinstall all applications and check for updates every time they run, which will result in the overwriting of previous data. But if the metadata of the file system can be identified, the deleted file system can possibly be restored. There is a risk associated with the directory analysis method as the integrity of the resultant data is compromised during the process of acquiring administrator privileges. The same caveat does not hold for the situation when the tools are used to collect data from the service provider's cloud as a legitimate communication protocol has been employed. Further the identification information obtained in most analyses employed by the authors carries a high degree of surety, as does the chip-off analysis.

Volatile memory forensics

Over the past decade the subfield of volatile memory forensics has evolved from a niche, specialist capability to become a reliable and effective technique for recovering forensically sound information from computer systems [53]. It has become an important source of evidence as contemporary computing applications make more use of memory to perform certain functions than was previously the case. Once data from memory has been acquired, the challenge is to interpret the raw memory into higher level artefacts. This is complicated by the absence of publicly available documentation of the internal structure of software, therefore requiring reverse engineering of the digital traces. But reverse engineering is time consuming, difficult to accomplish and it is not scalable. Several techniques and tools for memory forensics are now available, but generally the field is very much still in development. Although some of the tools are able to find evidence of malware, the techniques can generate vast amounts of data that are very time consuming to analyse.

The memory is a common site for cyber security attack by the injection of malware. For example, user space malware utilises code injection techniques to manipulate other processes or to hide its existence. Current tools, however, are unreliable when attempting to reveal the presence of malware in memory. Attackers can use a variety of methods to evade detection, for example, by creating an executable file that does not appear to be executable or by exploiting the paging mechanism. Some researchers are developing approaches that reveal all executable memory pages that might be of potential interest to an investigator, despite the use of hiding techniques [54].

Another commonly encountered problem when acquiring forensic memory from an active system is memory smear, which can occur especially when the system is under heavy load. Memory smear can result in corruption of a memory sample and difficulty in interpretation of the digital traces. Malware that targets memory can tamper with in-memory data. To address the issues of memory smear and tampering, strenuous testing of the memory parsing components of analysis frameworks must be conducted. Due to the large volumes and complexity of memory data, it is only feasible to conduct the testing automatically. Some researchers have developed a tool that they named *gaslight*which supports the seamless testing of memory forensic frameworks. *Gaslight* was able to find crashes in numerous core plugins for Linux and OS X, but not in Windows [55].

Currently available memory malware methods have improved, but the emerging challenges of malware in hidden memory and hypervisor-based malware can potentially impact their reliability. Computing vendors have structured memory so that it is divided into reserved and unreserved memory in order to perform different functions, with reserved memory generally avoided by forensic acquisition tools. Data can actually be hidden in the reserved areas and are often referred to as hidden memory. Hypervisor-based malware takes advantage of processor virtualisation that migrate a running system onto a virtual machine [56].

Additional work has been undertaken to look at the use of computer forensic processes to perform recovery of digital traces from graphics processing units (GPUs). Recovery of artefacts from GPUs is possible but subject to three major challenges: (1) the elusive global memory allocation scheme of GPUs, (2) varying levels of support for different GPU drivers and (3) the prerequisite for using certain types of operating systems and applications [57].

Dark net

The lack of privacy offered by digital communications was thrust into the public arena and became a vigorous global debate following the revelations revealed by the National Security Agency contractor, Edward Snowden concerning mass surveillance. Subsequently, the use of the Tor browser and network became mainstream around 2013 for members of the public and criminals alike. Tor is intended to protect the user from both network and local adversaries which is achieved through a design that obfuscates network activity and employs antiforensic techniques. Messages are encrypted in multiple layers. As the message passes through multiple nodes (thousands) in the Tor network, a layer of encryption is removed to reveal only the next node address until it reaches the final node and exits the network. The Tor browser bundle is an extended support release of Mozilla Firefox browser, a free internet browser that prioritises privacy and security and is available for download. Firefox, without the Tor extension, stores history, download and cookie information, which are very useful to the forensic investigator.

The increased popularity of the Tor browser has led to increased interest in research concerning the effectiveness in protecting users, including whether or not useful artefacts can be located during a forensic examination. Importantly, researchers have found that the use of the Tor browser is not as private as is widely believed. Without being too technical, it has been found that useful artefacts can be located:

(1) artefacts proving the installation and use of the browser are generated in memory and on the hard drive in the form of default bookmarks. The artefacts are attributable to a particular user, uniquely identify the Tor browser and will persist through the uninstallation and logout processes;
(2) when used on a Windows machine (as are most business and consumer computers) user activity is written to the Windows' registry as a consequence of recent updates to the Windows operating system, therefore revealing the titles of pages visited using the browser, and
(3) a forensic methodology to reveal Tor artefacts can be devised.

The information that can be revealed under static analysis (when the computer has been switched off) includes HTTP header information, web page titles and a URL. Under live analysis, traces of Tor process can be found after the browser had been closed and the user logged out. The path to the browser executable was visible in RAM and included the username and the device from which it was run [58]. Further, it has been found that, even after uninstalling the Tor browser bundle, logging out and the Tor-related processes had ended, Tor-related artefacts, including the absolute path to the Tor install directory, were detectable. Other artefacts can also be detected including the page title of visited websites suffixed with *Tor browser* and the absolute path to the Tor install directory, the username, reference to Firefox.exe within the browser directory and possible indications of the country in which the Tor exit node was located. In addition, artefacts can be recovered from unallocated space and considerable browsing data leakage can be forensically examined.

To the celebration of digital forensic examiners everywhere, it is apparent that the use of Tor on suspect computers is easily identified, it cannot be securely deleted and activity from the browsing session is determinable. The persisting Firefox.exe process could not be fully terminated by closing the browser window and exists in a traceable but inactive state. Further, Tor can be easily detected using live forensics, particularly when the browsing session is still active.

The conclusion that Tor writes browsing data to the hard drive means that the use of static forensics by forensic investigators is potentially more worthwhile than examining the contents of RAM, which was previously thought to be the only way of detecting Tor use. The vast majority of the browsing protocol can be located in the Windows' registry file, therefore making it possible for the activities of the user to be reconstructed.

As in many spheres of law enforcement investigation and intelligence, keeping an ear to the ground is a useful method of understanding what is happening in the public space and what fringe communities are thinking about. One useful forum to monitor is 'Reddit' which can reveal emerging trends in what people (Reddit users) are thinking about, especially when focusing on specific subreddits that attract specific communities of users. For example, an analysis of all posts on the subreddit 'darknet markets' examined the impact of a compromise to, or take down of, multiple international darknet markets in July 2017 found that the disposition of DarkNetMarkets subreddit users went from casual and relaxed to a state of concern, uncertainty and security mindedness. Words associated with law enforcement became highly relevant in many topics and the void left by the disablement of the previously most popular markets was filled by a multitude of newer and smaller markets [59].

The DarkNetMarkets community members revealed their concern about their trust for new markets and hackers which was evidenced by discussions concerning secure transactions between untrustworthy markets. Many discussions featured words referring to Bitcoin, drugs and delivery logistics. Cryptocurrency and security tools were consistent topics of conversation with the popular cryptocurrencies being Monero and Bitcoin plus there was also interest in VPN services. After the July takedown in which AlphaBay and Hansa were removed, the most relevant market name became Dream, along with additional markets named Aero, Agora, Traderoute, Sourcery, and Trishula in addition to decentralised market concepts such as OpenBazaar.

Discussion topics regarding cryptocurrency are a useful source of intelligence gathering for law enforcement as the discussions are not just restricted to security. To enhance anonymity, darknet market users often use additional services such as 'mixing' or 'tumbling' where users exchange cryptocoins with each other to increase the difficulty in tracing transactions. Although cryptocurrency providers will have multiple currency offerings for legitimate purposes, such as speculating and trading between currencies, some mixers have been successfully prosecuted. Some mixing services include Dash, Helix, Bitmixer (now taken down), Coinbase, Seraphim, LocalBitcoins, BitBay, Shapeshifter, and ViaBTC.

Users have now gone beyond only using Tor for anonymity and actively explore new systems to maintain anonymity and privacy. 'Tails' is currently the most recommended operating system to enhance operational security as it automatically configures software to connect to the Internet via Tor. Other operating systems include Whonix and Qubes. The sub-Reddit has also revealed an increased interest in virtual private networks (VPNs) with PureVPN the most relevant, authenticated and confidential communication with the subject of PGP encryption being discussed more frequently.

Topic modelling is a useful intelligence gathering technique from darknet markets and forums. Although not reviewed in this book, several references to topic modelling are provided and include the types of items being sold on AlphaBay and the top vendors [60]; dragnet hacker forums for source code, attachments, hacking tutorials [61]; malware [62]; and identifying topics on Chinese hacker forums which revealed new communication methods, specific security mechanisms and caution over faulty transactions [63]. Topic modelling has also been used to detect anxiety-related posts from multiple subreddits. As Reddit posts include usernames against posts, users exhibiting a behaviour of interest can be identified.

Antiforensics

To avoid detection, criminals, mischief makers and others who want their activities to remain unseen will often employ antiforensic techniques to obscure their activities to ensure that no trail of evidence is left behind. Antiforensics relates to the impeding of forensic processes by various means and can be defined as 'any attempts to alter, disrupt, negate, or in any way interfere with scientifically valid forensic investigations'. [64] Although there is considerable operational interest in this field for digital forensic examiners, that interest is not reflected in the research effort.

As of 2016 there were 308 listed and categorised antiforensic tools. Variables for each of the tools were described and included information such as the antiforensic capability, developing party, country of origin etc. Importantly, tools were included that were not designed for antiforensic purposes, but can be used with malicious intent. The taxonomy was designed to capture as many possible situations that a forensic examiner might encounter in the course of their work and is a useful guide for the examiner during the conduct of casework. Broadly, the taxonomy comprises the following classifications:

- *Data hiding* includes encryption, steganography, data contraception, file system manipulation, hard disc manipulation, memory hiding and network-based hiding. Each of these categories are further broken down into subcategories that provide considerable granularity. Most of the listed antiforensic tools fell into this category.
- *Artefact wiping* includes, but is not limited to, subcategories such as the wiping of files, removable disc, generic, registry and disk degaussing/destruction techniques.
- *Trail obfuscation* is the deliberate activity taken to disorient and divert a forensic investigation on a digital system or network. It includes P2P networking, IP address spoofing, data fabrication, data misdirection/misinformation and the use of a proxy server, among others. P2P networking software was found to be very prevalent.
- *Attacks against forensic tools and methods* includes alerts to forensic tool usage, antireverse engineering and hash value integrity attacks, among others. These tools have the potential to be the most devastating antidigital forensic activity in an investigation.

Useful analytical information regarding the antiforensic tools is maintained in a repository, including categorical data on the antiforensic tools plus the unique hash values related to the installation files of 191 publicly available antiforensic tools. The repository's 2780 unique antiforensic installation-related files are analysed for their presence in the National Software Reference Library. Of these, 423 distinct hashes were found to be in the 2016 Reference data set. The United States, Germany and Finland were the most prevalent source countries for antiforensics tools of those countries that could be identified.

Clearly there is a wide range of potential antiforensic techniques. In an inherently insecure network environment, cryptography and steganography have long been used to secure data communications. Cryptography is a well-established method to encrypt data legitimate and illegitimate purposes and for which there are many methods employed. It is always clear to an intermediary, for example, a digital evidence examiner, that a message has been sent and that encryption has been used. Cryptography is concerned with hiding the contents of the message, rather than hiding the message itself. Conversely, steganography is used to hide the message in a cover image and it is usually not apparent to an intermediary that a hidden message may be present. Steganography is concerned with hiding the existence of the message. The message recipient is able to extract the message from the image using a secret key. By also embedding an encrypted message inside an image, the message is doubly protected. There are over 140 different steganography tools using a variety of algorithms [65].

The simplest and most commonly used one is when the hidden message that is inserted into the coding for the pixels where it have least bearing on the colour of the image. When coding for colour, each pixel comprises 3 bytes, each of 8 bits that together total between 0 and 255. The colours are coded as follows, the position of each number representing red, green and blue, respectively: [66]

- black (0, 0, 0)
- white (255, 255, 255)
- red (255, 0, 0)
- green (0, 255, 0)
- blue (0, 0, 255)
- yellow (255, 255, 0)
- cyan (0, 255, 255)
- magenta (255, 0, 255)

For a demonstration of colour coding, see the RGB (red, green, blue) colour code chart [67].

Several methods have been developed to employ multiple security protocols to hide an obscured message. The most popular steganography method involves encrypting the message data and then the encrypted message is subjected to the hash-based least significant bit (H-LSB) method. This method embeds 8 bits of encrypted data in the least significant bit of the red, blue and green pixel values. By selecting the least significant bit of these pixel values, image quality will not be noticeably affected. This process is repeated until the entire message is embedded in the image. When the receiver is removing the encrypted message, the embedded data are sequentially removed in the order that it was embedded. Once removal is complete, the encrypted message can then be decrypted [68].

Similar techniques are used to embed encrypted messages in video using steganography and then employing lossless compression [69]. Lossless compression provides for a reduction in data size without any loss of data. Using video to securely hide data provides for better confidentiality and data recovery. The video stream is a series of images and sounds and any changes made by embedding data should be visually undetectable. Hiding an encrypted message in video will increase the volume of text that can be hidden.

Some believe that the earlier methods can cause detectable image distortion which will therefore compromise the security of messages. Other steganographic techniques will scatter the secret message code into randomised pixels or pixels where the image brightness changes sharply such as edge pixels. Most of the focus of steganographic techniques has been on English or similar languages. However, many languages other than English comprise characters that do not have American Standard Code for Information Exchange (ASCII) values,[h] with the characters represented by Unicode.[i] Once the font of another language is converted to Unicode format, the Unicode characters are converted to binary bits that can then be encrypted. As in other approaches the video file can then be converted into video frames, with each video frame then subjected to, for example, Canny edge detection to divide the image into edge and no edge pixel bits.

[h] http://www.asciitable.com.

[i] http://unicode.org/charts/.

The secret message bits are then embedded in the image. If the pixel is a nonedge pixel, then the image is hidden using the identical match technique, i.e. finding a pixel that has the same value as that of the secret message and then stored that position where it will match the secret message bits. Using the combined method the payload capacity is very high, and no distortion is visible to the human eye [70].

There exist multiple theoretical and practical methods that might be used to hide data and it is not feasible nor useful to canvass them here. To provide a flavour of the variety that might be available, a more obscure one is to use the ext4 file system that is used by Android and many Linux distributions. Within the data structure is the inode table which contains all of the metadata of a file or directory. Data that matches the normal internal structures of the inode table will not be recognised by digital forensic tools. For each file or directory in an ext4 file system, the following timestamps are provided: (1) last modification time; (2) last access time; (3) last metadata change, e.g. change of ownership, permissions or file size; (4) deletion time and (5) creation time. Notably the timestamps support nanosecond timestamps and although end users do not have visibility to that level of detail, it provides a capacity of a few megabytes in which to hide information. Of the five timestamps, the creation time is the only one that is not subject to change and is, therefore, suitable for hiding data. It has been found that a bitmap file of 357,574 bytes can be hidden and is indistinguishable from normal system usage as the timestamp distribution does not significantly deviate from a uniform distribution and the timestamps containing hidden information are indistinguishable from that of a normal file system operation.

It is recommended that the forensic examiner, in the absence of encryption, can use statistical analysis for pattern recognition to determine the presence of hidden messages. Other artefacts which might suggest an antiforensic technique have been used might be found in the log files or a nonsensical sequence of timestamps, such as access or modification states occurring before a file was created or just a few nanoseconds after creation and backup files that contain different timestamp information to the original [71].

Deleted and fragmented files

The concept of date and time in computing is an important consideration in digital forensics. As files are created, modified, deleted and overwritten, date/time events are important in the reconstruction of events that have taken place. Some deleted and fragmented files can provide useful evidence in the consideration of criminal activity. Although some attributes can be modified, the dates in the $FILE_NAME attribute can only be modified by the system kernel and are, therefore, immune from any known antiforensic tools [72].

A digital fragment is a remnant of a deleted file that resides in one or more contiguous sectors of a hard drive. A single file might leave several remnants in slack spaces which can be found in several ways. Slack spaces occur in various forms of which there are two main types: (1) Volume slack is the unallocated space left after creating a hard drive partition, and (2) file slack occurs in files that do not fully align with a multiple of a cluster size.

The physical allocation of files by the file system follows the rules of the applicable file system under which it is operating. For example, when a file in the NTFS file system (Microsoft) is deleted, the file record in $MFT table is marked deleted and the corresponding clusters are marked available in the system $Bitmap. The deletion event is recorded in the transaction journals, but none of the dates change in the $MFT drive. At this point, no dating is required and the file can be fully restored but without any guarantee for how long it will remain intact. The file record can be overwritten in two ways: (1) The record in the $MFT is allocated to a different file, but the file can be recovered by creating a new pointer to the file which will also create new system dates and (2) the available clusters are later allocated for a different file which results in overwriting of the file content. Many files also have a date contained within the file which can be used for fragment dating.

Dating file fragments is an important step for event reconstruction when deleted files form part of the evidence. The date of deleted files and file fragments can be determined with a high degree of accuracy. If the file created date is similar to the file modified date, then the file is intact and has not been modified. The dates of neighbouring files can be used to infer a minimum boundary for when a deleted file was created. Further the maximum date from the currently allocated file can be used to define the upper bound period for when the file was deleted. Together the minimum and the upper boundaries create a time window for a deleted file for which a fragment was found. The dating accuracy is affected by heavy usage of the hard drive, the frequency of defragmentation and the type of the file system that is in use.

Chip-off forensics

Chip off forensics is a technique used to extract data from memory in some circumstances, for example, when the tools available at the investigator's disposable do not support the device or the device is damaged and cannot be accessed by the tool. The devices concerned are usually mobile phones and other small portable devices, but the technique is increasingly useful for the forensic examination of IoT devices and drones. Chip-off is a technique in which the examiner directly interacts with the device hardware. The chip-off process involves the removal of the NAND flash memory chip from the device and the chip is then accessed directly to extract the raw data. The chip-off process for older devices is quite reliable as the number of raw bit errors was quite low. Advances in technology, however, have increased the storage capacity of NAND flash memory resulting in the number of raw bit errors increasing by several orders of magnitude. In normal use, modern NAND flash memory controllers employ sophisticated error-correcting codes which can correct raw bit errors. Consequently the standard chip-off method often cannot recover the data in modern NAND flash memory. Therefore the forensic process must also extract the error-correcting information, in addition to the raw data, that is stored within the chip controller and use this information to correct the errors [73].

In the interval between when the device is seized and the time that the investigator extracts the data, errors can be introduced as a result of charge leakage from the cells of the NAND flash memory (referred to as data retention errors). The traditional chip removal process is thermally based which can result in an increased number of introduced errors within the NAND flash memory by two to three orders of magnitude. The number of consequent errors might exceed the capacity of the error-correcting function. The chip-off procedure itself is quite destructive and can corrupt a large proportion of the data, therefore the technique is becoming less reliable as NAND chips are becoming more sophisticated. However, on the upside, more recent hardware-based approaches have been successful in reducing the number of errors resulting from the chip-off process. Flash memory manufacturers incorporate a *read-retry* mechanism in modern flash memory chips which significantly reduces the raw bit error rate. By incorporating the *read retry*-based error mitigation into the forensic data recovery procedure, the errors can be mitigated through the thermal-based chip removal and read procedure.

Social media

Social media is very much part of the fabric of contemporary society and with it comes further opportunities for bullying, harassment and other forms of aggression. In recent years, social media has provided a means of organisation for rebellion and the spread of misinformation with significant impacts on societal well-being and democratic processes. At a broader, more insidious level, social media has enabled state and nonstate actors to meddle in the government and social fabric of other countries, to troll to upset users and to provoke a response. At a local level in the United Kingdom, a survey of teenagers found that 41% respondents identified themselves as feeling depressed or helpless as a result of cyberbullying with a further 18% feeling suicidal [74]. Many families can relate to the experience of schoolyard bullying now moving into the privacy of the family home, which was once considered to be a sanctuary from daytime trauma.

The majority of police forces have been experiencing increased mentions of social media in crime reports. British police forces found around 16,000 mentions of Facebook and Twitter associated with crimes [75], while at around the same time, the Mid Ulster police found that only 17% of reports to police of harassment, abuse and threats resulted in an investigation [76]. Primary among the reports was Facebook which featured heavily.

The British House of Commons noted that social media platforms are being used to promote terrorism and murder by spreading propaganda and for recruitment to the ideological cause. In accepting the profits that the platforms generate, the platforms are neglecting their responsibility for the impact of the content that they are facilitating [77].

More recently, there has been an increase in hate speech, most notably a fivefold increase in race hate comments on social media following the United Kingdom's vote to leave the European Union [78]. It has been observed that almost a third of the world's population is active on Facebook alone, one social media platform of at least 65 available platforms worldwide. Social media platforms provide a place for individuals who are inclined towards racism, misogyny or homophobia can find a place that can reinforce their views and encourage them to act on their thoughts. Studies of the worldwide increase in violence attributed to online hate speech has found correlations between antirefugee Facebook posts and attacks on refugees; perpetrators of white supremacist attacks circulate among online racist communities, slurring and demonising of minorities, lynch mobs and vigilantism. Some government responses have included temporarily blocking access to social media platforms citing the lack of responsiveness from social media companies.

In international and domestic jurisdictions where sufficient legislation is in place and online behaviours transgress, identification of the offender is central to enforcement of the legislation. The volume of traffic is significant and conducting investigations and identifying offenders can be an impossible task, leaving victims vulnerable to sustained abuse. In particular, account holders can use false information to create a social media account on many platforms. Unattributable accounts are often created for the sole purpose of trolling and in recent times, bot accounts have been created for the same purpose. For most platforms an account can be created in seconds using a nondescript email account that provides no indication to the identity of the account owner. Although the account can be traced back to the email account provider, the investigation is reliant on the email service provider to provide information regarding the identity of the account holder. Most popular email service providers require a secondary means of identification such as a backup email account or a mobile phone number to verify the account. For some email service providers however, the backup information can be falsified.

Social media content and accounts can be deleted by the account holder, i.e. the owning offender. If the victim has not made a copy of the offending material, law enforcement is dependent on the service provider to have retained the material, retrieving it and providing it to law enforcement. It is recommended that a record is made of offending content as soon as it is identified as it may be the only chance to capture it before the offender deletes it. Critically, if an offender deletes their account, time is of the essence as the content can disappear quickly depending on the policies and management of the platform by the service provider. Law enforcement must obtain the legal authority to comply with the terms and conditions of the platform provider before the data can be provided. The challenge is that, in the intervening time, even if the victim records the offending material, the content, including the metadata, could be removed before law enforcement has had the opportunity to obtain the data. Most of the commonly used platforms provide guidance to law enforcement, including the processes for submitting a request for information, which will vary depending on the service provider and the jurisdiction. One such key process is a preservation order which will allow the service provider to store the evidence of potential criminal conduct pending a legal authority for disclosure. Generally, such a preservation will be for 90 days, but it can be for more or less time. The preservation order should be specific in terms of time interval and content regarding a specific account(s). Many social media service providers will advise the account holder that they are subject to a preservation order once it has been submitted.

The majority of social media platforms are based in the United States. Should a non-US agency require access to account information on one of these platforms, the processes for obtaining the information might not be straightforward. Mutual legal assistance is a process that can be used, although many countries are entering into bilateral arrangements, or treaties, that enable the simpler sharing and provision of account information but are dependent on the alleged offences under investigation.

Complete enforcement and regulation of social media platforms is beyond the capacity of law enforcement and is a shared responsibility of the platforms themselves. Further, within each jurisdiction, various charities and organisations exist that can provide guidance to victims of online abuse.

References

[1] IDG, 2018 Could computing survey, 14 August 2018, Retrieved from https://www.idg.com/tools-for-marketers/2018-cloud-computing-survey/.

[2] S. Liu, Global public SaaS market size 2008–2020, Statista (9 August 2019). Retrieved from https://www.statista.com/statistics/510333/worldwide-public-cloud-software-as-a-service/.

[3] NIST, Draft NISTIR 8006: NIST Cloud Computing Forensic Challenges, National Institute of Standards and Technology: NIST Cloud Computing Forensic Science Working Group, Information Technology Laboratory, 2014. Retrieved from https://csrc.nist.gov/csrc/media/publications/nistir/8006/draft/documents/draft_nistir_8006.pdf.

[4] R. Choo, M. Iorga, M. Herman, B. Martini, Cloud forensics: state of the art and future directions, Digit. Investig. 18 (2016) 77–78.

[5] V. Roussev, I. Ahmed, A. Barreto, S. McCulley, V. Shanmughan, Cloud forensics – tool development studies & future outlook, Digit. Investig. 18 (2016) 79–95.

[6] S. Mohtasebi, A. Dehghantanha, R. Choo, Cloud storage forensics: analysis of data remnants on SpiderOak, JustCloud, and pCloud, in: Contemporary Digital Forensic Investigations of Cloud and Mobile Applications, 2017, pp. 205–246 (Chapter 13).

[7] T. Dargahi, A. Dehghantanha, M. Conti, Investigating storage as a service cloud platform: pCloud as a case study, Contemporary Digital Forensic Investigations of Cloud and Mobile Applications. (Chapter 12), 2017, pp. 185–204.

[8] A. Dehghantanha, T. Dargahi, Residual cloud forensics: CloudMe and 360Yunpan as case studies, in: Contemporary Digital Forensic Investigations of Cloud and Mobile Applications, 2017, pp. 247–283 (Chapter 14).

[9] A. Amine Chelihi, A. Elutilo, I. Ahmed, C. Papadopoulos, A. Dehghantanha, An android cloud storage apps forensic taxonomy, in: Contemporary Digital Forensic Investigations of Cloud and Mobile Applications, 2017, pp. 285–305 (Chapter 12).

[10] R. Quick, K.-K.R. Choo, Big Digital Forensic Data, Volume 2: Quick Analysis for Evidence and Intelligence. Springer Briefs on Cyber Security Systems and Networks, Springer, 2018.

[11] B. Ogazi-Onyemaechi, A. Dehghantanha, R. Choo, Performance of android forensics data recovery tools, in: Contemporary Digital Forensic Investigations of Cloud and Mobile Applications, 2017, pp. 91–110 (Chapter 7).

[12] M. Petraitye, A. Dehghantanha, G. Epiphaniou, Mobile phone forensics: an investigative framework based on user impulsivity and secure collaboration errors, in: Contemporary Digital Forensic Investigations of Cloud and Mobile Applications, 2017, pp. 79–89 (Chapter 6).

[13] X. Lin, T. Chen, T. Zhu, T. Yang, F. Wei, Automated forensic analysis of mobile applications on Android devices, in: Digital Investigation: DFRWS 2018 USA – Proceedings of the Eighteenth Annual DFRWS USA, 26, 2018, pp. S59–S66.

[14] S. Nemetz, S. Schmitt, F. Freiling, A standardized corpus for SQLite database forensics, in: Digital Investigation: DFRWS 2018 Europe – Proceedings of the Fifth Annual DFRWS Europe, 24, 2018, pp. S121–S130.

[15] A. Ali, S.A. Razak, S.H. Othman, A. Mohammed, F. Saeed, A metamodel for mobile forensics investigation domain, PLoS One 12 (4) (2017).

[16] M. Guido, J. Buttner, J. Grover, Rapid differential forensic imaging of mobile devices, in: Digital Investigation, DFRWS USA 2016 – Proceedings of the 16th Annual USA Digital Forensics Research Conference, 18, 2016, pp. S46–S54.

[17] S. Saleem, O. Popov, I. Baggili, A method and a case study for the selection of the best available tool for mobile device forensics using decision analysis, Digit. Investig. 16 (2016) S55–S64.

[18] C. Jin, R. Wang, D. Yan, Source smartphone identification by exploiting encoding characteristics or recorded speech, Digit. Investig. 29 (2019) 129–146.

[19] AppBrain, Android and Google Play Statistics, 2020, Retrieved from https://www.appbrain.com/stats.

[20] X. Zhang, F. Breitinger, I. Baggili, Rapid Android parser for investigating DEX files (RAPID), Digit. Investig. 17 (2016) 28–39.

[21] M. Park, G. Kim, Y. Park, Lee, I. And Kim, J., Decrypting password-based encrypted backup data for Huawei smartphones, Digit. Investig. 28 (2019) 119–125.

[22] J. Clement, Internet usage worldwide – statistics & facts, Statista (25 July 2019). Retrieved from https://www.statista.com/topics/1145/internet-usage-worldwide/.

[23] I. Riadi, Sunardi, A. Fauzan, Examination of digital evidence on Android-based LINE Messenger, Int. J. Cyber-Sec. Digit. Forensics 7 (3) (2018) 336343. The Society of Digital Information and Wireless Communications.

[24] I. Riadi, R. Umar, A. Firdonsyah, Identification of digital evidence on Android's Blackberry messenger using NIST mobile forensic method, Int. J. Comp. Sci. Inf. Sec. 15 (5) (2018) 155–160.

[25] J. Van Zandwijk, A. Boztas, The iPhone health app from a forensic perspective: can steps and distances registered during walking and running be used as digital evidence? Digit. Investig. 28 (2019) S126–S133.

[26] T. Alyahya, F. Kausar, Snapchat analysis to discover forensic artifacts on android smartphone, in: The 7th International Symposium on Frontiers in Ambient and Mobile Systems. Procedia Computer Science, 109C, 2017, pp. 1035–1040.

[27] S. Liao, Kik ap won't shut down after acquisition by MediaLab, CNN Business (19 October 2019). Retrieved from https://www.cnn.com/2019/10/19/tech/kik-messenger-saved/index.html.

[28] K. Ovens, G. Morison, Forensic analysis of Kik messenger on iOS devices, Digit. Investig. 17 (2016) 40–52.

[29] S. Wu, Y. Zhang, X. Wang, X. Xiong, L. Du, Forensic analysis of WeChat on android smartphones, Digit. Investig. 21 (2017) 3–10.

[30] A. Marfianto, I. Riadi, WhatsApp messenger forensic analysis based on android using text mining method, Int. J. Cyber-Sec. Digit. Forensics 7 (3) (2018) 319–327. The Society of Digital Information and Wireless Communications.

[31] P. Onovakpuri, Forensic analysis of Skype, Viber and WhatsApp messenger on android platform, Int. J. Cyber-Sec. Digit. Forensics 7 (2) (2018) 119–131.

[32] A. Jayakrishnan, V. Vasanthi, Empirical survey on advances of network forensics in the emerging networks, Int. J. Cyber-Sec. Digit. Forensics 7 (1) (2018) 38–46.

[33] A. Caesarano, I. Riadi, Network forensics for detecting SQL injection attacks using NIST method, Int. J. Cyber-Sec. Digit. Forensics 7 (4) (2018) 436–443.

[34] R. Davies, The Internet of Things: Opportunities and Challenges, The European Parliament Research Service, 2015. http://www.europarl.europa.eu/RegData/etudes/BRIE/2015/557012/EPRS_BRI(2015)557012_EN.pdf.

[35] I. Yaqoob, I. Hashemite, T. Ahmed, A. Kazmi, C. Hong, Internet of things forensics: recent advances, taxonomy, requirements, and open challenges, Futur. Gener. Comput. Syst. 92 (2019) 265–275.

[36] P. Fremantle, P. Scott, A security survey of middleware for the internet of things, PeerJ (2015). PrePrints [Online] https://peerj.com/preprints/1241v1/.

[37] A. Cassidy, The "Internet of Things" Revolution and Digital Forensics, 2014. https://www.nuix.com/2014/02/19/the-internet-of-things-revolution-and-digital-forensics.

[38] J. Gubbi, R. Buyya, S. Marusic, M. Palaniswami, Internet of Things (IoT): A vision, architectural elements, and future directions, Futur. Gener. Comput. Syst. 29 (7) (2013).

[39] O. Yakubu, O. Adjei, B.C. Narenda, A review of the prospects and challenges of internet things, Int. J. Comput. Appl. 139/10 (2016). http://www.ijcaonline.org/research/volume139/number10/yakubu-2016-ijca-909390.pdf.

[40] R.C. Hegarty, D.J. Lamb, A. Attwood, Digital evidence challenges in the internet of things, in: International Workshop on Digital Forensics and Incident Analysis, 2014. https://www.cscan.org/openaccess/?id=231.

[41] F. Servida, E. Casey, IoT forensic challenges and opportunities for digital tracers, Digit. Investig. 28 (2019) S22–S29.

[42] R. McKemmish, What is forensic computing, Trends Issues Crime Crim. Justice 118 (1999). http://www.aic.gov.au/media_library/publications/tandi_pdf/tandi118.pdf.

[43] S. Thomas, K.K. Sherly, S. Dija, Extraction of memory forensic artifacts from Windows 7 RAM image, in: IEEE Conference on Information and Communication Technologies, 2013.

[44] J. Gantz, D. Reinsel, The Digital Universe in 2020: Big Data, Bigger Digital Shadows, and Biggest Growth in the Far East, International Data Corporation, 2012. https://www.emc.com/collateral/analyst-reports/idc-the-digital-universe-in-2020.pdf.

[45] E. Oriwoh, D. Jazani, G. Epiphaniou, Internet of things forensics: challenges and approaches, in: Proceedings of the 9th IEEE International Conference on Collaborative Computing: Networking, Applications and Worksharing, 2013.

[46] F. Servida, E. Casey, IoT forensic challenges and opportunities for digital traces, Digit. Investig. 28 (2019) S22–S29.

[47] N. Ellouze, S. Rekhis, N. Boudriga, M. Allouche, Cardiac implantable medical devices forensics: postmortem analysis of lethal attackers scenarios, Digit. Investig. 21 (2017) 11–30.

[48] A. Nieto, R. Rios, J. Lopez, IoT-forensics meets privacy: towards cooperative digital investigation, Sensors 18 (2) (2018) 492.

[49] G. Horsman, Unmanned aerial vehicles: a preliminary analysis of forensic challenges, Digit. Investig. 16 (2016) 1–11.

[50] A. Dennon, The Best Voice Assistants, Reviews.com, 16 July 2019. Retrieved from https://www.reviews.com/voice-assistant/.

[51] H. Chung, J. Park, S. Lee, Digital forensic approaches for Amazon Alexa ecosystem, in: DFRWS 2017 USA - Proceedings of the Seventeenth Annual DFRWS USA. Digital Investigation, 22, 2017, pp. S15–S25.

[52] W. Jo, Y. Shin, Kim, D. Yoo, D. Kim, C. Kang, J. Jin, J. Oh, B. Na, T. Shon, Digital forensic practices and methodologies for AI speaker ecosystems, in: Digital Investigation: DFRWS 2019 USA – Proceedings of the Nineteenth Annual DFRWS USA, 29, 2019, pp. S80–S93.

[53] B. Schatz, M. Cohen, Editorial: advances in volatile memory forensics, Digit. Investig. 20 (2017) 1.

[54] F. Block, A. Dewald, Windows memory forensics: detecting (in)intentionally hidden injected code by examining page table entries, in: Digital Investigation: DFRWS 2019 USA – Proceedings of the Nineteenth Annual DFRWS USA, 29, 2019, pp. S3–S12.

[55] A. Case, A. Das, S.-J. Park, J. Ramanujam, G. Richard, Gaslight: a comprehensive fuzzing architecture for memory forensics, in: Digital Investigation: DFRWS 2017 USA – Proceedings of the Seventeenth Annual DFRWS USA, 22, 2017, pp. S86–S93.

[56] R. Palutke, F. Freiling, Styx: countering robust memory acquisition, in: Digital Investigation: DFRWS 2018 Europe – Proceedings of the Fifth Annual DFRWS Europe, 24, 2018, pp. S18–S28.

[57] Y. Albabtain, B. Yang, The process of recovering image and web page artifacts from the GPU, Int. J. Cyber-Sec. Digit. Forensics 7 (2) (2018) 132–141.

[58] M. Muir, P. Leimich, W. Buchanan, A forensic audit of the Tor browser bundle, Digit. Investig. 29 (2019) 118–128.

[59] K. Porter, Analyzing the DarkNetMarkets subreddit for evolutions of tools and trends using LDA topic modeling, Digit. Investig. 26 (2017) S87–S97.

[60] J. Grisham, Barreras, C. Afarin, M. Patton, H. Chen, Identifying top listers in Alphabay using Latent Dirichlet Allocation, in: 2016 IEEE Conference on Intelligence and Security Informatics, 2016.

[61] S. Samtani, S. Chinn, H. Chen, Exploring hacker assets in underground forums, in: 2015 IEEE International Conference on Intelligence and Security Informatics, 2015.

[62] I. Deliu, C. Leichter, K. Franke, Extracting cyber threat intelligence from hacker forums: support vector machines versus convolutional neural networks, in: 2017 IEEE International Conference on Big Data, 2017.

[63] Z. Fang, X. Zhao, Q. Wei, G. Chen, Y. Zhang, Y. Xing, C. Li, H. Chen, Exploring key hackers and cybersecurity threats in Chinese hacker communities, in: 2016 IEEE Conference on Intelligence and Security Informatics, 2016.

[64] K. Conlan, I. Baggili, F. Breitinger, Anti-forensics: furthering digital forensic science through a new extended, granular taxonomy, Digit. Investig. 18 (2016) S66–S75.

[65] Steganographic Software, Retrieved from, 2020. http://www.jjtc.com/Steganography/toolmatrix.htm.

[66] SlideServe, The art and science of writing hidden messages steganography, 2020, Retrieved from https://www.slideserve.com/sissy/the-art-and-science-of-writing-hidden-messages-steganography.

[67] RapidTables, RGB color codes chart, 2020, Retrieved from https://www.rapidtables.com/web/color/RGB_Color.html.

[68] A.M. Abdullah, R.H.H. Aziz, New approaches to encrypt and decrypt in image using cryptography and steganography algorithm, Int. J. Comput. Appl. 0975-8887, 143 (4) (2016) 11–17.

[69] R. Apau, J.B. Hayfron-Acquah, F. Tuwm, Enhancing data security using video steganography, RSA and Huffman Code Algorithm with LSB Insertion, Int. J. Comput. Appl. 0975-8887, 143 (4) (2016).

[70] B. Chandel, S. Jain, Gurumukhi text hiding using steganography in video, Int. J. Comput. Appl. 0975-8887, 142 (6) (2016).

[71] T. Gobel, H. Baier, Anti-forensics in ext4: on secrecy and usability of timestamp-based data hiding, Digit. Investig. 24 (2018) S111–S120.

[72] A. Bahjat, J. Jones, Deleted file fragment dating by analysis of allocated neighbors, Digit. Investig. 28 (2019) S60–S67.

[73] A. Fukami, S. Ghose, Y. Luo, Y. Cai, O. Mutlu, Improving the reliability of chip-off forensic analysis of NAND flash memory devices, Digit. Investig. 20 (2017) S1–S11.

[74] Vodafone, Ground-breaking Vodafone survey reveals 43% of teens think cyber bullying a bigger problem than drug abuse, 2015, Retrieved from https://www.vodafone.com/news-and-media/vodafone-group-releases/news/groudbreaking_global_survey.

[75] M. Evans, Police facing rising tide of social media crimes, Daily Telegraph (June 5, 2015). Retrieved from https://www.telegraph.co.uk/news/uknews/crime/11653092/Police-facing-rising-tide-of-social-media-crimes.html.

[76] Tyrone Times, Mid Ulster police face rising tide of social media crime, August 23, 2015, Retrieved from https://www.tyronetimes.co.uk/news/mid-ulster-police-face-rising-tide-of-social-media-crime-1-6918145.

[77] House of Commons, Home Affairs Committee Report 8 – Radicalisation: the counter-narrative and identifying the tipping point, 2016.

[78] Z. Laub, Hate Speech on Social Media: Global Comparisons, Council on Foreign Relations, June 7, 2019.

Cryptocurrency

14

The forensic analysis of cryptocurrencies presents their own unique challenges to the examiner. In recent years the understanding of these payment systems has improved for consumers and for examiners. Cryptocurrencies appeal to criminals to facilitate their nefarious conduct due to three key features: (1) ensuring limited anonymity in which users might only reveal their identity either negligently or might be revealed by other parties who use external data to match transactional data that is visible in the public ledger, (2) independence from a central authority in which rules are made by consensus, rather than imposed by the central authority, that cannot be abolished or regulated by force, and (3) double spending attack protection where the owner of cryptocurrency cannot use the same units to pay two different recipients. As of January 2016 there were over 600 cryptocurrencies that have since grown to 1596 as of 1 April 2018 and 9914 markets available in which to trade the currencies [1,2]. The proliferation of cryptocurrencies and their markets represents an impossible task for law enforcement and regulating authorities to monitor proactively.

Cryptocurrency is distinct from electronic money. Electronic money refers to money that exists in banking computer systems that may be used to facilitate electronic transactions. It is backed by fiat currency and is primarily used for electronic transactions. There is a growing acceptance of cryptocurrency in conventional transactions, which characteristically

1. does not require a central authority;
2. retains an overview of cryptocurrency units and their ownership through a public ledger;
3. defines whether new units can be created, the circumstances in which they are created, their origin and how to determine their ownership;
4. exclusively and cryptographically proves ownership of the units;
5. allows transactions in which ownership of the units changes; and
6. performs, at most, one transaction when simultaneous instructions for changing ownership are received.

Cryptocurrency uses a peer-to-peer system to store transactions within a blockchain database. The blockchain is a public ledger, maintains a record of every transaction and is available to anyone within the network. Cryptocurrencies can be owned through cryptocurrency accounts that comprise a combination of a private key and a cryptocurrency address. A weakness in the Bitcoin system is that the account address can be calculated from the private key. There is no limit on the number of attempts at guessing the password.

There are four levels of anonymity for cryptocurrency accounts:

- Transparent account where the owner has revealed their identity in a credible manner.
- Semitransparent account is traceable by the appropriate government administration.

Strategic Leadership in Digital Evidence. https://doi.org/10.1016/B978-0-12-819618-2.00014-0

- Pseudoanonymous account owner can only be known to the owner's business partners, which might not include knowing the owner's name, but the business partners are in possession of information that can lead to ascertaining the owner's identity.
- Anonymous account owner is unknown to anyone but the owner.

The anonymity of cryptocurrencies is determined by a seemingly random set of alphanumeric characters with no known association to the legal entity. When used in conjunction with Tor and a virtual private network, the entity's identity is protected. Transactions can be further obscured by 'mixers' who take coins from different sources and redistribute them to hide the original owner of the coin and the transactions with which they are involved. This can be taken a step further by breaking coins up into smaller bits before redistribution. These features have made cryptocurrencies perfectly attractive for criminal transactions has been used to facilitate sex trafficking, drugs, guns, fake identity, assassination, financing terrorism, tax evasion, identity theft, money laundering, malware (such as ransomware) and child abuse.

Each country has chosen how to, or not, regulate the trading of cryptocurrencies within its borders. Some countries have banned cryptocurrencies from operating or trading entirely but often with little impact. It is noted that, at this point in time, transactions occurring outside of conventional systems will generally result in a loss of revenue to the state as transaction fees, such as taxes, are unable to be collected. Cryptocurrencies are not subject to the usual financial levers that governments can use to control the economy. Conversely the lack of control and transparency allows legitimate users to purchase goods and services electronically and protects them from criminal actors who may seek to control the local economy.

As criminal organisations change their approach to one of exploiting the characteristics of cryptocurrencies, an understanding of the digital traces that are indicative of transactions in the blockchain is essential in order to conduct a robust and effective digital forensic analysis and interpretation. This is especially so when cryptocurrency is used to transact between criminal groups.

Investigating global currencies has specific requirements beyond those that have traditionally been part of the investigator's and digital forensic examiner's tool kits. The tools are not restricted to technical tools, but will also require legislative permission to make enquiries of other jurisdictions. As cryptocurrency transactions are maintained on a public ledger, the seeking of special permissions from financial institutions are not required. In addition, there is a range of computer and mobile applications available to users to assist in the management of their cryptocurrency holdings. Knowledge of the applications, how and where they store the data is important, especially if the applications encrypt or hide the data.

When conducting a digital forensic investigation, the usual digital forensic steps should be taken to ensure that all evidence is collected

- Acquire the random-access memory (RAM) using the specific tools for this purpose and with which the examiner is familiar. The RAM will help to determine if the data is encrypted, which programmes are running, applications that might contain necessary artefacts and an indication of additional connected devices.

- Locate any wallets which contain artefacts of cryptocurrency. The wallets might contain transactional information with timestamps. They can be tracked and used to identify people or groups and disclosed during litigation.
- Artefacts are stored on the drive in different locations according to the file system in use and depend on the purpose of the device in the currency exchange. For example, the device might be unknowingly used for currency mining or it might be encrypted to hide transactions. Logs of Internet searching can also identify other entities in the actor's network.
- Network traffic can be captured which can reveal transactional data, the IP addresses of collaborators and online shopping sites for illegal goods and services.

Tools are emerging that assist to identify illegal activity using digital currencies. The tools use public blockchain data with known addresses of threat actors to track the usages of currency and will increase in capability and reliability.

References

[1] J. Lansky, Possible state approaches to cryptocurrencies, J. Syst. Integr. 9 (1) (2018) 19–31.

[2] D. Orr, D. Lancaster, Cryptocurrency and blockchain: a discussion of forensic needs, Int. J. Cyber-Sec. Digit. Forensics 7 (4) (2018) 420–435, and The Society of Digital Information and Wireless Communications.

Crime types in the digital realm 15

Crime that involves digital technology is often regarded as something relatively new and somewhat mysterious, whereas it is actually a relatively simple concept. In this chapter, I will try to simplify computer crime by identifying the similarities with 'conventional' crime and explain some of the differences. Cybercrime can be classified into two categories based on the means of the attack, which may inform responsibilities and resource allocation with an organisation:

- cyber-enabled crime comprising traditional crimes that are increased in scale or boundary by the use of digital technology,
- cyber-dependent crime comprising offences for which a digital technology is required, that is, they are usually perpetrated against a computer or a system that holds information.

Sometimes, the distinctions between the classifications can become blurred when considering various actions within a criminal investigation. For example, a Trojan that might be used to infect a banking computer system to perpetrate a fraud can, of itself, be a crime in addition to the function for which it has been purposed. In this example, the use of the Trojan, although it used to facilitate a crime type (fraud), can also be considered to be a crime tool, that is, a means by which to achieve an end rather than being an end itself.

The immediate challenge of investigating crime in the digital realm is the classification of the criminal conduct. Crime in the digital realm is still relatively new and jurisdictions will classify crime according to their own definitions, which may or may not be consistent with those of their neighbours. Further, the cybercrime domain itself will have variations in the use of terminology. These factors will lead to confusion and misrepresentation within organisations and in communication with stakeholders. For example, virus and worms are well-defined technical terms based on the functionality of the code, whereas spyware, although usually referred to as a nefarious action, is software that monitors computer activity for both licit and illicit purposes.

The use of technology is not predetermined, but technology has interpretive flexibility, that is, it can be interpreted and used in different ways, depending on the needs of the user group. A given technology will become embedded in a community which has a shared understanding of how the technology is to be used. Technologies will become part of the social structure and culture of the community, such as that of a criminal enterprise and they will shape the organisational structures, cultural beliefs and practices within the community.

A simple example is the use of mobile devices. While the use of mobile devices is ubiquitous within the community at large, a criminal enterprise might specifically choose to use burner phones to communicate or to use smartphone communication apps that employ end-to-end encryption. The use of specific technology and procedures becomes normalised within the community.

Strategic Leadership in Digital Evidence. https://doi.org/10.1016/B978-0-12-819618-2.00015-2

As previously described in the Introduction and elsewhere in this book, digital evidence is ubiquitous within the criminal environment where it can function as a witness (often a passive and/or silent witness), a victim or a tool to the criminal activity. There are differences of opinion as to how criminal actions in the digital realm are classified and defined in part because they do not stand still and continue to evolve over time. For example, previous definitions have categorised cybercrime as cyber-enabled crime (traditional crimes that are increased in scale and penetration by the use of digital technologies) and cyber-dependent crimes (crimes that can only be committed using digital technology). The distinction between cyber enabled and cyber dependent, while of esoteric interest, is not especially meaningful to people operating in the real world and solving real-world problems, for example, the investigation of an offence. The chief of police and the minister will not be interested in whether the activity is cyber enabled or cyber dependent, but will be more interested in questions such as whether or not an offence was committed, the extent of harm to the victim, adequacy of the relevant legislation, the identification and detention of the perpetrator, whether or not this is a new and emerging trend and do we have the capability to deal with it? The critical questions are related to the motivation and intent of the actions, associations and reference to crime tools and crime types. The crime types involving cybercrime are largely unchanged over time and are subject to the motivation and intended consequences of an action. The tools that are used to perpetrate the intended criminal action can be digital in nature in the same way as they can be for some other technology or physical device. For example, a crowbar has a legitimate useful purpose for which it was designed, but it also might be used in a burglary.

Technology can be considered to be an extension of the human being. Individuals have a certain set of capabilities and capacity that is defined and limited by their own mental and physical capacity and the environment in which they are located. Employing technology can extend this capacity to meet the individual's intentions and motivation by augmenting their existing capacity or by introducing new capabilities. This section briefly describes some criminal activities that are classified as 'cybercrime', that is, where technology is used in the commission of the crime irrespective of the crime is 'enabled' or 'dependent' by technology.

Technologies that might be used in perpetrating a crime will be defined by the capabilities that require extension. This discussion is limited to the scope of digital evidence, although other technologies are often also used. Technologies might be employed for the following purposes, but are not limited to

- obtaining information for planning purposes through the use of protocols, imaging equipment, eavesdropping equipment and hacking tools,
- disabling of security systems by interfering with signals and hacking tools,
- transporting actors to and from the crime scene using a motor vehicle,
- coercing persons, to ensure that they assist or do not interfere with the criminal activity, through the use of compromising information and images,
- communication between members of the criminal enterprise using mobile phones, computers etc.,
- cybercrime or online crime through the use of software tools and services for accessing computer networks, causing damage and stealing information.

Technologies that might be used to avoid detection and escaping punishment include, but are not limited to

- preventing, altering, destruction, concealment and falsification of evidence through the use of disposable or encrypted communication devices, data erasing and anonymising tools,
- securing escape using mobile phones and creating false digital trails.

There are several attractions of digital technologies to the conduct of criminal action. One such attraction is the inherent lower risk to the perpetrator of being detected and apprehended. For example, over recent decades, there is a reduced frequency of armed robberies of banks which is, no doubt, due to the hardening of banks as targets which has, therefore, increased the potential risk to perpetrators. But this has shifted the risk profile for criminals as, in hardening the physical banks, there is now a much lower risk to perpetrators by attempting to obtain funds online. Another attraction of digital technologies that appeals to perpetrators is the transnational environment of cybercrime. Interjurisdictional boundaries can be exploited by criminals to avoid detection and prosecution and can also provide a greater number and range of potential targets. Criminal groups might establish a presence in one country with the specific intention to target victims in another country in the knowledge that local law enforcement is uninterested as the local citizens are not being targeted.

With certain skills that are not especially difficult to obtain, would be perpetrators in developing economies now have the access and opportunity to target wealthy potential victims residing in developed economies. For example, it has been estimated that, as of 2014, there were over 800,000 perpetrators of advanced fee scams worldwide.

Cybercrime prevalence

The UK National Crime Agency and Strategic Cyber Industry Group identified that cybercrime accounts for 53% of all crime in the United Kingdom [1, 2]. The UK Office for National Statistics estimated there were 2.46 million cyber incidents and 2.11 million victims of cybercrime in 2015. The cybercriminal market where criminal expertise and cybercrime tools are developed is available for a price that can be purchased by those who are motivated, yet less skilled to conduct their criminal activity. Despite the figures in the preceding text, the National Crime Authority believes that there is a significant degree of underreporting.

Cybercrime security breach or attack

The UK National Crime Agency noted that 43% of businesses within the United Kingdom experienced at least one cyber security breach or attack in 2017, although it is widely believed that it is underreported, with the figure rising to 64% for medium-sized businesses and to 72% for large businesses. The NCA also notes that such criminal acts can adversely impact on national prosperity, therefore impacting the whole population [3]. It is becoming increasingly difficult to distinguish between those attacks perpetrated by crime groups and those perpetrated by nation states.

Whereas in the past a security breach conducted through the use of malware might have been the sole motive for the attack, a security breach is now usually regarded as the means to performing some other nefarious activities. Cyberattack is now part of the armoury of organised crime groups, state actors, industrial espionage and conflict. Malware attacks are no longer restricted to computers but are now also targeted to mobile phones with the number of attacks estimated at 116.5 million attacks in 2018, up from 66.4 million attacks in 2017. The rise in the number of attacks is despite a reduction in the number of unique malware files, indicating that the quality of '...mobile malware has become more impactful and precise'. [4]

Those who create malware are becoming increasingly professional, fee for service providers for customers to use for which they are then recompensed. The professionalisation of malware production has led to the development of a marketplace where those who wish to do so can purchase an attack. An example is ZeuS, a banking Trojan, which was available for sale from online forums. ZeuS was able to use a range of methods for stealing data which were then used to access bank accounts and transfer funds. The malicious code was available for American, British, Canadian and Germans banks with a sliding, yet moderate, pricing structure based on the number of the potential victims.

Cyberbullying, violence and harassment

Cyberbullying has been recognised since the early 1990s and refers to an intentional act that uses information and communication technologies against a victim. The acts can be perpetrated through text, mobile phone, cyberstalking and cybergrooming using a range of tools including email, chat, instant messaging and social media [5]. The end result can be a young victim of cyberbullying eventually succumbing to taunts and suggestions that she/he kill herself/himself. It is contended that a generic mobile digital forensic readiness solution used to monitor secondary school students' devices could mitigate bullying by appropriately allowing an intervention based on the content of text messages. In order to intervene, the forensic capability would be required to be in a readiness position that maximises the use of potential digital evidence while minimising the cost of the investigation. Although there are obvious privacy concerns over monitoring devices, it can be argued that, in some jurisdictions, there is some legal precedence for content monitoring on mobile devices as several courts have determined that organisations should have been aware of the flagrant abuse that was occurring within their domain. Children's parents are influential in this discussion as they expect and demand that there is control over what their children are exposed to. Monitoring can be actioned by installing a mobile agent that monitors the mobile user's activities and transmits them to secure storage for analysis. If the analysis reveals nefarious intent, an alert is generated and early intervention can be actioned. With the current rapid developments in data analytics and artificial intelligence, the ability to identify abusive material and alert appropriate authorities, including parents, in real time is a distinct possibility.

Illicit drugs and pharmaceuticals

Although the sales of illicit substances still occurs in the physical world, there is an increasing volume of sales over the Internet. Silk Road, the infamous Internet site on the darknet that could only be accessed via Tor and only accepted Bitcoin transactions for the purchase of goods, was famously taken down by the FBI in October 2013 [6]. It was replaced by Silk Road 2.0 only to be shut down by the FBI and Europol in November 2014. It was a site where illicit drugs, firearms, child abuse material and other illegal goods and services could be purchased anonymously. As anticipated, Silk Road was replaced, and, by 2016, there were approximately 100 darknet markets and vendor stores selling goods and services similar to those previously offered by Silk Road [7–9]. The prevalence of darknet markets has continued to grow. The Wall Street Market and Silkkitie (aka the Valhalla Marketplace) were closed down in May 2019 through international collaboration between several agencies. At the time the Wall Street Market was regarded as the second largest illegal darknet market with 5400 registered sellers and 1.1 million user accounts with drugs estimated to comprise 60%–70% of its trade [10].

Of the eight most popular marketplaces, the vast majority of the listings were for drugs with the majority being cannabis derivatives, stimulants and ecstasy analogues. A significant proportion of the listings were for larger amounts implying that many dealers were using the online markets as their supplier for later offline sale. It is estimated that darknet markets generated total monthly revenue of $12–$21 million in January 2016. Several million dollars more of revenue can be included if prescription drugs, alcohol and tobacco are included. Most vendors are in the United States (890) followed by the United Kingdom and Germany. Intercontinental trade is common with many vendors shipping to Australia and New Zealand.

As Internet security continues to develop, increasing numbers of buyers and sellers are feeling confident in evading detection. Not only are drug purchases available on the darknet but also on numerous web shops easily found by search engines where designer drugs, labelled as, for example, 'research chemicals', can also be purchased. There are four broad modes of detection and intervention of drug market places, including the traditional techniques in the drug chain, postal detection and interception, online detection and online disruption.

Child exploitation

Child exploitation is perhaps the crime type that is most impacted by digital technology, most notably the production and dissemination of child abuse images. In recent years, most, if not all, jurisdictions have enacted laws and conventions that define and prohibit images, including videos, of child sexual abuse and various related activities, with many jurisdictions extending their reach to include their own citizens who perpetrating crimes against children extraterritorially. The number of persons charged for various offences within this crime type has been steadily increasing over the past two decades, although it is believed that the majority of offences continue to remain undetected.

Offenders are usually members of groups who have a mutual interest in child abuse and are generally aware of the legal and social ramifications that would result from their offending if they are caught. Consequently the more skilled offenders are likely to escape detection through the obscuration of their identity and behaviour by using various means such as antiforensic tools, encryption and anonymised communication systems such as peer-to-peer, Tor and darknet. Lesser skilled offenders are more likely to be caught and prosecuted than those who are technologically advanced. In addition to the affirmation and enhancement of an individual's illicit interests through cognitive distortion, group membership will provide access to technical instruction on observation and the avoidance of detection provided by other members of the group.

The use of technology changes the dynamic between offenders and victims in comparison with offences committed in the physical world, as the offending takes place remotely. In the physical world, investigations are initiated as a result of attention being drawn from the victim, a family member, a friend or an associate rather than directly by law enforcement. When online offences occur, it is usually uncovered as a result of law enforcement detection, intelligence and monitoring on online networks, although referrals can also be received through other means of discovery, such as an incidental discovery during computer repair. Moreover, there is likely to be an association between offenders who possess child exploitation material and also commit contact offences. Another key difference between child exploitation online and that which occurs in the physical world is the phenomenon of 'once it is on the net, it is on the net forever'. Victims will become aware, if they are not already, that their images of abuse are on the Internet and can be downloaded repeatedly. Each download of exploitative images represents another incident of abuse and furthers the victimisation.[a]

Forensic examination of digital evidence will provide useful, multifaceted and relevant information that can assist the investigation to identify offenders, victims, locations and other pertinent factors such as financial transactions. Information can be derived from the devices and storage media, images, videos, audio, text and metadata. The digital traces can reveal details such as identifying characteristics of both the victim and the offender, age, physical description, gender and distinguishing marks and can inform the severity of abuse. The International Child Sexual Exploitation Database contains over 1.5 million images and videos and has assisted in the identification of over 19,400 victims and over 8897 offenders [11].

Prostitution

Prostitution is thriving and continuing to grow through the use of the Internet for marketing to new clients and avoiding detection by law enforcement. The anonymity pro-

[a] It should be noted that possession and distribution of images do have real-world impacts in that the dissemination of child abuse images creates and reinforces a market for such material, which then incentivises the production of further original material. Some child abuse networks are sophisticated with defined structures and rules and may include rules requiring the continuous contribution of original child abuse material in order to maintain membership and/or to ascend to higher levels within the organisation.

vided by new technologies and websites is easily exploited by the sex trade. Further, targeted enforcement of the Internet appears to have limited potential for policing. The purveyors of sex use coded language comprising hidden meanings not only on covert web sites but also on legitimate websites [12]. Researchers from Michigan State and Loyola University Chicago found that 80% of all sales of sex now occur online [13]. Purveyors have also developed apps that assist in locating a prostitute who is nearby the client based on location data. Notably, law enforcement has the capacity only to target the most egregious cases of exploitation with a primary focus on sex trafficking and minors. The use of websites by both prostitutes and potential customers has changed the nature of traditional street walking prostitution, including the sharing of information of potential police investigations in order to minimise the risk of arrest.

Following the shutdown of the notorious Backpage website which, at the time, was regarded as the largest prostitution marketplace and policy changes at Craigslist to remove the 'Personals' and 'Therapeutic Services' categories from its listings, purveyors of sex for sale have diversified in their use of technology to conduct business. Various platforms and apps are now used and are quite often geographically specific in their use. Some platforms are used to contact vulnerable underage girls to offer them the opportunity to make money very quickly and a range of platforms and apps are used to market services with coded references to 'massage' and 'pleasant experiences'. Some of the platforms and apps that are commonly used by pimps to recruit sex workers and victims and/or to advertise services include Facebook, Tinder, Snapchat, Instagram and WhatsApp. But the use of technology does not end there. The explosion in availability of sex robots and sex dolls, often representing children, has provided new opportunities for abuse, including brothels offering both human and sex robots for abuse [14].

Sexting

Sexting refers to the transmission of sexually explicit material, such as images and video, via a messaging app. The primary criminal concern is when underage children and teenagers are involved. Of broader concern, although not criminal in most jurisdictions, is sexting in other environments, such as in the workplace or between colleagues, when the images are unwanted. Unwanted sexting might have administrative implications, such as harassment, in workplace and employment contracts.

Digital technologies have enabled individuals to write and send hurtful and threatening messages, harass others by sending or posting embarrassing videos and images, therefore causing emotionally damaging experiences. The real-world harm to the victim can include feelings of fear, humiliation, shame and anger.

People trafficking

People trafficking is moving from the streets to social media. The Internet and, increasingly, smartphone apps, such as dating sites and gaming sites, are widely used by people traffickers for recruiting victims. Victims are forced into sex trafficking through domestic servitude in schemes that typically have a high involvement of organised crime. Some trafficked persons, especially children, have been reportedly forced to commit criminal and terrorist acts such as arson or to serve as scouts. The platforms are not only used for recruitment but also used to trade the trafficked persons between traffickers. In some countries the traffickers can comprise local community leaders, religious leaders and former trafficking victims who have graduated to become perpetrators. Vulnerable people, mostly women and girls, are lured by fraudulent or misleading job opportunities that are advertised on the Internet, some of which appear on legitimate employment websites. A number of jurisdictions have increased their investment in digital evidence capability in recent years to detect, investigate and prosecute trafficking in humans.

Terrorism

It has been well established that terrorist groups are adept users of cyber technology to further their aims and they continue to develop their capability. Many terrorist group activities are conducted in the cyber realm and employ many different platforms including promoting their cause, disseminating propaganda, recruitment and planning as well as using cyber technology as a weapon to attack enemies. The Internet provides many benefits to terrorists including fast communication, instant accessibility, ease of use, opportunities for publicity, anonymity, cost-effectiveness and transnational capability, thus reinforcing their strengths in an asymmetric conflict.

Many of the popular social media platforms are being used as platforms for terror activities, most notably the recent killing of 51 people in Christchurch, New Zealand on 15 March 2019. The incident was live streamed on Facebook and was first reported to Facebook by a user 12 min after the live stream had ended. It was viewed approximately 4000 times before Facebook was able to remove the video and Facebook removed approximately 1,500,000 copies of the video in the first 24 h following the incident. By then, it had made its way onto other social media platforms and often in modified form to escape automated detection. The New Zealand Prime Minister, Jacinda Ardern, noted that although the ideas and language of division have existed for a long time, the methods of distribution and organisation of those ideas are new. By the time that New Zealand Police had alerted Facebook to the existence of the video, it had already been posted to 8chan, an online message board and home to some of the most vitriolic content on the Internet that enjoys minimal moderation [15, 16]. 8chan's byline is 'Welcome to 8chan, the Darkest Reaches of the Internet', but 8chan is only welcoming of those persons who would be considered to be on the fringe. [17] It is suspected that the 8chan was the host of the gunman's manifesto.

Terrorist acts in cyberspace can be classified into four categories: (1) information attacks where the objective is to access, steal, modify or destroy information or data in targeted systems. This can include distributed denial-of-service (DDOS) attacks against, for example, government institutions which serve to undermine public confidence in institutions; (2) material damage to critical infrastructure, such as communications, transportation and utilities; (3) facilitation of conventional attacks by obtaining information about critical infrastructure such as building plans and layouts and the addresses of critical entities and (4) financial and propaganda activities including the solicitation of donations, advertising products and events to collect fees; and the distribution of propaganda to promote the terrorist group's activities and assist in the recruitment and radicalisation of members and potential members [18].

Corruption

The widely publicised 'Panama Papers' arose from a leak to the International Consortium of Investigative Journalists (ICIJ). Together with more than 100 media partners, 11.5 million documents exposed the offshore holdings of world political leaders, links to global scandals and the hidden financial dealings of fraudsters, drug traffickers, politicians, prominent persons in sports and other celebrities. The firm at the centre of the investigation created shell companies and corporate structures for the ownership of assets. The documents analysed by the ICIJ included emails, financial spreadsheets and corporate records totalling 2.6 terabytes. Using collaborative platforms, 400 journalists across 80 countries working in 25 languages indexed, organised and analysed the data [19].

Fraud

The widely held view is that crime rates have been falling over the past two decades throughout the developed world, but the reduction cannot be adequately and universally explained by increased effectiveness through enhanced security and crime prevention strategies. One school of thought is that the digitalised world has created new opportunities for criminal activity but is difficult to accurately measure. The opportunities to engage in fraud have become substantially enhanced, both in volume and sophistication, through the use of technology. It is estimated that there were 3.3 million frauds perpetrated in the United Kingdom in the year to June 2018, at a total cost of £160 billion to the economy. Of these, 84% of frauds are reportedly cyber related [20]. The numerous technological advances over the past two decades have contributed to the enhanced opportunities to commit fraud, including an increased volume of Internet users and their availability, social media, online shopping, online banking and online commerce. In short, individuals make their personal information, including identity, tax, banking details, family and friendship circles and assets available online and, therefore, available to be exploited.

A significant change in victim of crime demographics has occurred as a result of increased digitalisation. Whereas, previously, the most likely victims of crime were young males, an attractive target now for potential fraud is an older person. An older person is likely to have funds available, such as life savings, pension fund, assets and access to bank funds such as a line of credit. In short, technology has made committing fraud much easier. Technology provides access to a much larger pool of potential victims, with a reduced chance of getting caught and prosecuted and with substantially greater potential rewards. Furthermore, in general, law enforcement organisations have not met the challenge of the changing crime profile, reflected by the increase in fraud, with adequate resources and training. As fraud, especially that perpetrated online, is difficult to measure (it is estimated that 80% of fraud in the United Kingdom goes unreported), law enforcement has been reluctant to proportionately realign resources to address the problem. Further, there is a systemic reluctance at the political and agency levels to acknowledge the prevalence of fraud, instead favouring the narrative of an apparent decline in crime incidents as reflected by crime statistics [21]. In reality, it appears that rather than a decline in crime, there is actually a shift in crime to that which is less measured.

Romance fraud

The expansion of online dating and social media has created the opportunity for romance fraud. It usually involves a person creating a false identity, or profile, or stealing the legitimate identity of another person. Victims are enticed with the possibility of establishing a genuine relationship with a potential suitor. Once trust is established between the parties, the victim is groomed and presented with scenarios that pressure them to send money. A scenario might include money for hospital treatment for a sick relative or a business opportunity.

Advanced fee

Advanced fee frauds, such as the well-known Nigerian 419 scams, occur where a potential victim is presented with an 'opportunity' to pay a small amount of money up front in return for a larger amount at a later time. The opportunities can include inheritances, which the perpetrator will promise to share with the victim, once the victim has provided some funds to, for example, pay the taxes to release the inheritance, fantastic business and investment opportunities and corrupt or 'unjustly persecuted' officials seeking assistance in the movement of funds, through the prepayment of taxes or other charges. The low cost of accessing the necessary technology means that emails can be sent to millions of recipients, of which only a small percentage of whom respond and make the scam worthwhile. Other inducements can include foreign lotteries that require a release fee, holidays that can be purchased online or software that provide greater surety and profits for gambling.

Environmental fraud

The highly publicised scandal concerning the circumventing of emission regulations for diesel-powered vehicles sold by Volkswagen Group emerged in September 2015.

Illegal software was installed on Volkswagen motor vehicles that could detect when the vehicles were being tested for emissions and respond by changing their performance to improve results. Volkswagen has admitted to 11,000,000 cars worldwide having the illegal software installed, with legal action being taken in several jurisdictions [22].

Copyright infringement

Copyright infringement continues to be very popular among cybercriminals. The world's largest BitTorrent distribution site, KickassTorrents (KAT), launched in 2008, operates by providing *.torrent* and *.magnet* links so that users can download unauthorised copies of copyright material. The site does not host the infringing material itself, but it is estimated to have distributed over $1 billion of copyright material by 2016. To evade law enforcement, KAT moved the Internet domains around the world. The administrator of the site was arrested in July 2016 on charges of criminal copyright infringement, conspiracy to commit money laundering and conspiracy to commit copyright infringement at which time the site was taken down. His advertising revenue was estimated at $12 million per year [23]. By December 2016, the former KAT staff revived the KAT community with a website bearing the same look and feel as the original site.

A group of hackers were charged with intellectual property theft following a hack into the computer systems of film production companies and the theft of digital files, including feature films, trailers, episodes of television series and audio tracks. The defendants changed the properties of the computer files to make them easier to distribute online, then offered the stolen movies for sale via private communications. Some of the stolen material was uploaded onto pirate movie websites and a PayPal account was used to receive and distribute proceeds from the sale of the stolen movies. The group comprised individuals residing in the United Kingdom, India, United Arab Emirates and Malaysia [24].

Theft of intellectual property and confidential business information

The nature of intellectual property theft has changed markedly. Businesses primarily now store their intellectual property and run their business processes on information systems. Without adequate security, malevolent employees and nefarious others will seek access to the business information and download it for economic advantage. In one example a Chinese national and US permanent resident allegedly stole trade secrets concerning the research and development of the downstream energy market product from a US-based petroleum company [25]. In another example, two Chinese members of a hacking group known as *Advanced Persistent Threat 10* (APT10 Group) and working for a company called *Huaying Haitai Science and Technology Development*, which was associated with the Chinese Ministry of State Security, were charged with global intrusions that were committed over more than a decade. They were alleged to have committed computer intrusions, conspired to commit wire fraud and aggravated identity theft. Their modus operandi was to target the intellectual property, confidential business and technological information of business service providers that manage the information technology infrastructure of businesses and governments around the world. More than 45 companies in a wide range of industries were targeted, including aviation, satellite and maritime technology, industrial factory automation, automotive supplies, laboratory instruments, banking and finance, telecommunications and consumer electronics, computer processor technology, information technology services, packaging consulting, medical equipment, healthcare, biotechnology, pharmaceutical manufacturing, mining and oil and gas exploration and production. The APT10 Group were alleged to have hacked into companies in at least 12 countries [26].

Cyberstalking

The Internet has enabled stalking to be conducted more easily and efficiently by those who choose to do so. For example, a woman from Florida, United States, pled guilty to cyberstalking and sending threatening communications online. She had created and used at least 369 Instagram accounts and 18 email accounts to cyberstalk, harass or intimidate six former colleagues and associates by email, phone calls, text messages and social media messages [27].

In another example, using Internet applications to hide his identity, a New York man conducted extensive harassment against three victims including threatening the female and harassing two males. In addition, he framed the victims for crimes and workplace violations that they had not committed that included sending a false tip to the Department of Homeland Security that accused the female of smuggling drugs. Although the truth was eventually revealed, agents spent more than 1000 hours investigating the case [28].

A man from Seattle, Washington, United States, was found guilty of conducting cyberstalking and threat campaigns against several people including death threats, body shaming and hate speech. For the first victim the man posted fake profiles, on dating sites, professing an interest in sadomasochistic and underage relationships. The profile included the victim's contact details and photographs which resulted in solicitations and harassing messages from strangers. This was particularly disturbing for the victim as he worked for a nonprofit youth organisation. The defendant registered a second victim, a female, for several weight loss and suicide prevention programs which resulted in calls and emails from various weight management and suicide prevention organisations. He then began sending anonymous death threats to her by email [29].

Identity theft

Not withstanding the willingness of individuals to make their personal and private details public, notably, through social media, but also in providing commercial entities with similar information, there is an increasing concern over an individual's right to privacy and the integrity of one's identity. Critically the action of consent is critical to the notion of privacy. The Universal Declaration of Human Rights (1948) determined that the right to privacy is a human right.

However, digitalisation has afforded tremendous opportunity for data and privacy-related crime. Not only can an individual's information, such as bank statements, credit cards, social security or other state identification credentials, correspondence etc., be made available, but also is the similar type of information of the individual's contacts. Identity theft has now become a major criminal industry with various methods used to perpetrate it. The key developments that facilitate the violation of privacy, therefore leading to identity theft, include the mass collection and collocation of personal information, the ability to process and manage personal information, pervasive encryption and increasingly sophisticated malware. Identity theft can be used in three ways to cause harm to a victim: (1) impersonation of the victim to open new accounts, (2) to obtain products and services or (3) to take over the victim's account(s).

A commonly used method to obtain identifying information is to use phishing. In a typical phishing attack, a sender will send an email that appears to be from an authoritative person or a person known to the receiver that requests identifying information. On receipt of the requested information, the information will be used for ulterior purposes. For example, a group of accomplices sent emails to employees of a school system requesting tax information for the school system's employees. The information was used to file electronic tax returns in the names of the victims of the scheme and claimed refunds totalling $491,737 [30].

Following his arrest in Maldives during 2014, a Russian national was convicted and sentenced to 27 years in prison on 38 charges including 9 charges of hacking and 10 charges on wire fraud. He had intruded into the payment systems of hundreds of businesses over a period of 15 years and had 2.9 million unique credit card numbers in his possession when he was arrested. He stole $170 million and was ordered to return this amount in restitution to businesses and banks that were victims [31].

Identity theft has now taken on a more sinister edge. Individuals can purchase credit card details, often in bulk, from websites on the darknet. Such websites are marketplaces for stolen credit cards, personal credentials and user identities and password combinations that can then be used to conduct criminal activity. Some websites will offer free samples and frequent user discounts.

Revenge pornography

The newly emerged and legislated crime of involuntary or revenge pornography is becoming better understood. Dedicated websites that publish intimate images of, often, spurned lovers have been shut down and the administrators prosecuted. The impact on victims can be severe with careers destroyed and families torn apart and in several instances has led to suicide. Legislation that prohibited the involuntary posting of intimate images that has been available to law enforcement in the United

Kingdom was strengthened in 2015 [32]. As of March 2020 46 states, the District of Columbia and one territory within the United States have legislation making involuntary pornography a punishable crime. In 2015 the administrator of UGotPosted.com was sentenced to 18-year imprisonment after being convicted under Californian legislation [33].

Advertising fraud

The Internet is largely free to use due to paid digital advertising. Website owners display advertising material for which they receive fees from companies who pay to have their goods and services advertised to consumers. Digital advertising revenue is based on how many users click or view ads on the website. Using botnets an international criminal group was alleged to have committed wide-scale digital advertising fraud. The individuals built complex, fraudulent digital advertising infrastructure to mislead and defraud companies by faking users and webpages. The group used botnets to control and direct computers to load advertisements on fabricated webpages in order to fraudulently obtain digital advertising income.

The criminal group operated a purported advertising network and had business arrangements with other advertising networks to receive payments for placing ad tags on websites. The ad tags, however, were not placed on legitimate publishers' websites, but were instead placed on fabricated websites that were hosted on 1900 rented computer servers located in commercial data centres. Ads were loaded onto fabricated websites that spoofed over 5000 domains. The deception was further enhanced by giving the appearance that human users were interacting with the websites by programming the data centre servers to simulate the Internet activity of human users by browsing the Internet through a fake browser, using a fake mouse to move around and scroll a webpage, starting and stopping a video player and falsely appearing to be signed into Facebook. The group also loaded 650,000 IP addresses, assigned multiple IP addresses to each server and then registered those same IP addresses to give the appearance that the data centre servers were residential computers belonging to human Internet users who were subscribed to consumer Internet providers. Using this scheme, businesses paid more than $7 million for advertising that was never viewed by a human.

In a second scheme, some of the individuals of the group used a global botnet network of malware infected computers which were operated without the owners' knowledge or consent. The group developed a sophisticated command and control system to direct and monitor the infected computers and to check whether or not an infected computer had been identified by cybersecurity companies as being associated with fraudulent activity. The group accessed more than 1.7 million infected computers, owned by businesses and individuals in several countries, by using hidden browsers to download fabricated webpages and load ads onto those webpages. This second scheme falsified billions of ad views and businesses paid over $29 million for ads that were never viewed by humans [34].

Ransomware

Ransomware is a relatively new cybercrime but has quickly become prominent with several notable and high-profile cases occurring since 2017. A ransomware payload will encrypt a system and demand payment, invariably in the form of a cryptocurrency. When payment is made, the encryption key is released and the data can be restored [35]. Organised crime has found that ransomware is a very useful way to meet their goals. One common example is *WannaCry* which is a worm that infects Windows computers and encrypts files on the hard drive rendering them inaccessible. It then demands a ransom payment in Bitcoin (to avoid identification of the perpetrators) to decrypt them. *WannaCry* exploits a vulnerability in the Windows Server Message Block protocol which helps nodes on networks communicate. It quickly garnered a high level of attention due to the high-profile targets including the UK National Health Service, leading to the postponement of thousands of operations [3]. It is also interesting as it is widely believed that the Windows vulnerability was discovered by the US National Security Agency who developed a code to exploit it, called *EternalBlue*. *EternalBlue* was then stolen by hackers and released in a post on 8 April 2017. *WannaCry* uses *EternalBlue* to infect computers and even though Microsoft released a patch for the vulnerability, many systems remained vulnerable [36].

Money mule

Money mule scams, often using gift cards or wire transfers, are often initiated and facilitated through digital communications. The lure is often related to online dating, work-at-home jobs or prizes that do not actually exist. Scammers send money to the victim, sometimes by cheque, asking for a portion of it to be forwarded to someone else. The method of forwarding is usually in the form of gift cards or wire transfers. The victim might deposit the cheque, which might be a fake cheque and if the funds have been expended, the bank will seek the funds to be returned by the victim. Some victims might also provide their personal banking details which will enable the scammer to misuse the bank account.

Summary

As can be seen, with ubiquitous digitalisation in all facets of human contemporary lives, including in private, government and business, there is a huge volume and range of opportunity for criminals to exploit technology. Importantly, it is not the devices that criminals are after, but the data that devices contain or provide access to. Data, the oil of the 21st century, are of inestimable value when exploited both for good and for evil. The types of crime that have been described in this chapter represent a broad range of activities that reach into almost every corner of human existence, every activity in which a person might be engaged.

References

[1] D. Swinhoe, Cybercrime More Prevalent than Traditional Crime in UK, IDG Connect, 21 July 2016. http://www.idgconnect.com/abstract/18829/cybercrime-prevalent-traditional-crime-uk. Accessed 24 July 2016.

[2] National Crime Authority, NCA Strategic Cyber Industry Group: Cyber Crime Assessment, http://www.nationalcrimeagency.gov.uk/publications/709-cyber-crime-assessment-2016/file, 2016. Accessed 23 July 2016.

[3] Home Office, Serious and Organised Crime Strategy. Her Majesty's Government, Retrieved from, https://assets.publishing.service.gov.uk/government/uploads/system/uploads/attachment_data/file/752850/SOC-2018-web.pdf, 2018.

[4] Kaspersky, Number of mobile malware attacks doubles in 2018, as cybercriminals sharpen their distribution strategies, Retrieved from, https://usa.kaspersky.com/about/press-releases/2019_number-of-mobile-malware-attacks-doubles?PID=6361382&CJ_CID=3486349&CJ_PID=6361382&CJ_CID_NAME=Future%20Publishing%20Ltd&utm_source=CJ&utm_medium=affiliate&CJEVENT=da2007ab5fd-f11ea811d04320a240613&utm_campaign=6361382, 5 March 2018.

[5] V.R. Kebande, N.M. Karie, S. Omeleze, A mobile forensic readiness model aimed at minimizing cyber bullying, Int. J. Comput. Appl. 140/1 (2016). http://www.ijcaonline.org/research/volume140/number1/kebande-2016-ijca-909193.pdf. Accessed 28 July 2016.

[6] S. Gibb, Silk Road underground market closed – but others will replace it, Retrieved from, https://www.theguardian.com/technology/2013/oct/03/silk-road-underground-market-closed-bitcoin, 3 October 2013.

[7] Kruithof, K., Aldridge, J., Decary-Hetu, D., Sim, M. Dujso, E. and Hoorens, S. Internet-facilitated drugs trade: an analysis of the size, scope and the role of the Netherlands. Rand Europe, Published by the RAND Corporation, Santa Monica, CA, Cambridge, UK. (2016). Retrieved from, http://www.rand.org/content/dam/rand/pubs/research_reports/RR1600/RR1607/RAND_RR1607.pdf. Accessed 10 August 2016.

[8] T. Mendelsohn, Darknet drug dealers rake in millions each month, Arstechnica (2016). Retrieved from, https://arstechnica.com/tech-policy/2016/08/darknet-drug-dealers-are-making-millions-each-month/. Accessed 15 August 2016.

[9] J. Stone, How many darknet marketplaces are there? Approximately 100, Cyberscoop (May 6, 2019). Retrieved from, https://www.cyberscoop.com/dark-web-marketplaces-research-recorded-future/.

[10] M.J. Schwartz, Darknet disruption: 'Wall Street Market' closed for business, Bank Info Security (May 3, 2019). Retrieved from, https://www.bankinfosecurity.com/darknet-disruption-wall-street-market-closed-for-business-a-12446.

[11] Interpol, International Child Sexual Exploitation Database, Retrieved from, https://www.interpol.int/en/Crimes/Crimes-against-children/International-Child-Sexual-Exploitation-database, 10 March 2020.

[12] Allocca, S. Online prostitution thriving via social media. Forensic Magazine. (2016) Retrieved from, http://www.forensicmag.com/article/2016/08/online-prostitution-thriving-social-media?et_cid=5471402&et_rid=454862972&location=top&et_cid=5471402&et_rid=454862972&linkid=http%3a%2f%2fwww.forensicmag.com%2farticle%2f2016%2f08%2fonline-prostitution-thriving-social-media%3fet_cid%3d5471402%26et_rid%3d%%subscriberid%%%26location%3dtop Accessed 17 August 2016.

[13] Finn, M. and Henion, A. Prostitution Has Gone Online – And Pimps Are Thriving. MSUToday Michigan State University. (2016) Retrieved from, http://msutoday.msu.edu/news/2016/prostitution-has-gone-online-and-pimps-are-thriving/?utm_campaign=-media-pitch&utm_medium=email Accessed 17 August 2016.
[14] Fondation Schelles, Sexual exploitation: new challenges, new answers. 5th global report, Retrieved from, http://fondationscelles.org/pdf/RM5/5th_Global_Report_Fondation_SCELLES_2019_download.pdf, 2019.
[15] M. Flynn, No one who watched New Zealand shooter's video live reported it to Facebook, company says, Wash. Post (March 19, 2019).
[16] E. Stewart, 8chan, a nexus for radicalization for the Poway and Christchurch shooters, explained, Vox (May 3, 2019). Retrieved from, https://www.vox.com/recode/2019/5/3/18527214/8chan-poway-synagogue-shooting-christchurch-john-earnest.
[17] 8chan, Retrieved from, https://8ch.net/index.html, July 14, 2019.
[18] M. Conway, L. Jarvis, O. Lehane, Terrorist's Use of the Internet: Assessment and Response, IOS Press, 2017.
[19] ICIJ Staff, The Panama Papers: About this project, Retrieved from, https://panamapapers.icij.org/about.html, April 2016. Accessed 22 August 2016.
[20] Clifford Chance, Cyber-enabled crime highlighted as key risk area for financial and economic crime in the NCA's 2019/20 Annual Plan, Retrieved from, https://www.cliffordchance.com/hubs/regulatory-investigations-financial-crime-insights/our-insights/cyber-enabled-crime-highlighted-as-key-risk-area-for-financial.html, 29 April 2019.
[21] M. Button, C. Cross, Technology and fraud: the 'fraudogenic' consequences of the Internet revolution, in: Routledge Handbook of Technology Crime and Justice, 2017.
[22] R. Hotten, Volkswagen: the scandal explained, BBC News (10 December 2015). Retrieved from, http://www.bbc.com/news/business-34324772. Accessed 17 August 2016.
[23] Farivar, C. Alleged founder of world's largest BitTorrent distribution site arrested. n.d. Retrieved from, http://arstechnica.com/tech-policy/2016/07/kickasstorrents-alleged-founder-artem-vaulin-arrested-in-poland/ Accessed 16 August 2016.
[24] Central District of California, Members of international movie piracy ring indicted in scheme to steal and sell pre-release Hollywood films and TV shows, U.S. Department of Justice: U.S. Attorney's Office, December 12, 2018. Retrieved from, https://www.justice.gov/usao-cdca/pr/members-international-movie-piracy-ring-indicted-scheme-steal-and-sell-pre-release.
[25] Office of Public Affairs, Chinese National Charged with Committing Theft of Trade Secrets, U.S. Department of Justice: Justice News, December 21, 2018. Retrieved from, https://www.justice.gov/opa/pr/chinese-national-charged-committing-theft-trade-secrets.
[26] Office of Public Affairs, Two Chinese Hackers Associated with the Ministry of State Security Charged with Global Computer Intrusion Campaigns Targeting Intellectual Property and Confidential Business Information, U.S. Department of Justice: Justice news, December 20, 1998. Retrieved from, https://www.justice.gov/opa/pr/two-chinese-hackers-associated-ministry-state-security-charged-global-computer-intrusion.
[27] Middle District of Florida, Pasco Woman Pleads Guilty to Cyberstalking and Making Threats Online, Department of Justice: U.S. Attorney's Office, December 21, 2018. Retrieved from, https://www.justice.gov/usao-mdfl/pr/pasco-woman-pleads-guilty-cyberstalking-and-making-threats-online.
[28] Eastern District of Virginia, New York Man Sentenced to Prison for Cyberstalking, Department of Justice: U.S. Attorney's Office, December 21, 2018. Retrieved from, https://www.justice.gov/usao-edva/pr/new-york-man-sentenced-prison-cyberstalking.

[29] Office of Public Affairs, Seattle man sentenced to over two years in prison for cyberstalking campaign, U.S. Department of Justice: Justice news, December 7, 2019. Retrieved from, https://www.justice.gov/opa/pr/seattle-man-sentenced-over-two-years-prison-cyber-stalking-campaign.

[30] District of Connecticut, Nigerian National Pleads Guilty of Role in Phishing Scheme that Victimized Connecticut School Employees, Department of Justice: U.S. Attorney's Office, 2018. Retrieved from, https://www.justice.gov/usao-ct/pr/nigerian-national-pleads-guilty-role-phishing-scheme-victimized-connecticut-school.

[31] M. Bellisle, Russian man sentenced to 27 years in U.S. cybercrime case, Forensic Magazine (April 4, 2017). Retrieved from, https://www.forensicmag.com/news/2017/04/russian-man-sentenced-27-years-us-cybercrime-case.

[32] C. Farivar, Congresswoman introduces revenge porn bill, setting max penalty at 5 years, arsTECHNICA (2016). Retrieved from, http://arstechnica.com/tech-policy/2016/07/congresswoman-introduces-revenge-porn-bill-setting-max-penalty-at-5-years/. http://arstechnica.com/tech-policy/2016/07/congresswoman-introduces-revenge-porn-bill-setting-max-penalty-at-5-years/. Accessed 16 August 2016.

[33] J. Mullin, "Revenge porn" in UK now punishable by two years in prison, arsTECHNICA (2015). Retrieved from, http://arstechnica.com/tech-policy/2015/04/revenge-porn-in-uk-now-punishable-by-two-years-in-prison/. Accessed 22 August 2016.

[34] United States Attorney's Office, Eastern District of New York, Two International Cybercriminal Rings Dismantled and Eight Defendants Indicted for Causing Tens of Millions of Dollars in Losses in Digital Advertising Fraud: Global Botnets Shut Down Following Arrests, United States Department of Justice, November 27, 2018. Retrieved from, https://www.justice.gov/usao-edny/pr/two-international-cybercriminal-rings-dismantled-and-eight-defendants-indicted-causing.

[35] D. Orr, D. Lancaster, Cryptocurrency and the blockchain: a discussion of forensic needs, Int. J. Cyber-Sec. Digit. Forensics 7 (4) (2018) 420–435.

[36] J. Fruhlinger, What Is WannaCry Ransomware, How Does It Infect and Who Is Responsible, CSO, August 30, 2018. Retrieved from, https://www.csoonline.com/article/3227906/what-is-wannacry-ransomware-how-does-it-infect-and-who-was-responsible.html.

Investigations

16

'My life is in my phone'

The purpose of this chapter is to point to where digital evidence might be located and to take into consideration the role that digital evidence might play in an investigation, if any at all. The purpose is not to advise as to how an investigation should be conducted. After all, this is not a book about investigations, and there are many people far more qualified than I who can advise as to how an investigation should be conducted. Moreover, every investigating and intelligence organisation has its own doctrine for investigation and/or gathering and analysing intelligence.

'My life is in my phone' is often my opening line when I am speaking with people who do not have any expertise in digital evidence and are naive to its implications. To put it another way, when I leave home in the morning and if I have my phone, my keys and my wallet, I am good for the day as these items provide me with access to everything that I need. Increasingly, there is less need for my wallet as most purchases via credit card(s) attached to the phone or payment details stored on a website. The car keys and house keys are going the same way as the wallet.

For most people, everything they think, say and do, their relationships with family, friends, colleagues, associates, institutions, service providers and, dare I say it, the government, will be evidenced or referenced by a digital trace. An individual's smartphone, computer and other electronic devices, such as a home speaker, implanted medical devices or motor vehicle, not only are access devices to the Internet and repositories of their own personal and business data and information but also are also an access to their thoughts, state of well-being and activities. The digital traces can, perhaps, reveal more about a person than even those who are closest to them.

The first principle of forensic science as articulated by Edmond Locard in 1920 and later expressed by Kirk:

> *Wherever he steps, whatever he touches, whatever he leaves, even unconsciously, will serve as a silent witness against him. Not only his fingerprints or his footprints, but his hair, the fibres from his clothes, the glass he breaks, the tool mark he leaves, the paint he scratches, the blood or semen he deposits or collects. All of these and more, bear mute witness against him. This is evidence that does not forget. It is not confused by the excitement of the moment. It is not absent because human witnesses are. It is factual evidence. Physical evidence cannot be wrong, it cannot perjure itself, it cannot be wholly absent. Only human failure to find it, study and understand it, can diminish its value [1].*

Although the aforementioned was written to apply to physical evidence, it has become clear that the principles equally apply to digital evidence. In any human endeavour, there is most likely to be a digital trace that evidences or refers to that activity.

Strategic Leadership in Digital Evidence. https://doi.org/10.1016/B978-0-12-819618-2.00016-4

Digital technology can have an involvement in crime and therefore be a potential source of digital evidence, in up to three ways:

1. Technology is used as an aid in committing crime.
2. Technology has contributed to the emergence of crime.
3. Technology is a witness to crime.

The recurring theme in this book is that consumer and business technology continues to evolve rapidly. The advances in technology continue to produce greater diversity and options in which citizens can go about their daily lives to accomplish their daily business objectives, interact with family and friends, and in their entertainment and relaxation. This diversity also presents an array of opportunities for criminals to engage in nefarious activities and in which digital traces of their activities can be recorded.

Building on the statistics and progressions earlier in this volume, there are particular trends in the technology market that will impact on investigations and should be taken into consideration in any planning for an investigation involving digital evidence. Such information concerning the activities of persons and involved in criminal activity, including suspects, victims and witnesses, should then be made known to the examiners conducting the digital forensic examination to ensure that relevant evidence is not accidentally excluded from the examination processes.

If financial transactions are relevant to the investigation, even if they are of peripheral relevance, such as placing a particular user in front of the screen, data that are relevant to such transactions or the consideration of such transactions should be included in the examination. For example, the e-commerce industry sells approximately $3.45 trillion in goods and services [2] with digital interactions influencing $0.56 of every dollar spent in a bricks and mortar store [3]. Importantly, 88% of online shoppers visited online showrooms or participated in web rooms before visiting a physical store [4]. The majority of online consumers prefer to use digital self-service tools such as chatbots when making enquiries and this preference is expected to increase in prevalence in the future. A significant proportion of online purchasers who own a smart speaker have used the smart speaker to purchase online and it is expected that voice searches will comprise half of all future Internet searches.

The e-commerce segments that have generated the most sales are travel ($750 billion), fashion ($525 billion), electronics ($393 billion), toys and hobbies ($386 billion) and furniture and appliances ($273 billion).

Contributing further to the complexity of the digital lake, the hardware used in places of business is becoming increasingly diverse. A business might provide its people with desktop and notebook computers, but an increasing proportion of organisations are being impacted by more advanced technology such as mobile devices and the employee-friendly policy of 'bring your own device', often referred to as BYOD. Although organisations usually provide desk phones for their people, business is increasingly being conducted using mobile phones and unified communications, such as chat via desktop or notebook.

Transparency

An indisputable principle of law enforcement is ensuring public confidence in the policing service. In an environment of rapid technological change in the business and personal markets, there is a vast range of information, much of it personal and private, that is accessible to law enforcement and other government agencies. When law enforcement accesses such information or deploys technology for the purposes of effectiveness, efficiency, accountability and the assessment thereof, the public experiences a degree of discomfort. There are many reasons for this phenomenon, often based on the history of the jurisdiction in question, which might have included the misuse of personal and private information by the government. In many Western democracies, for example, as espoused by the founding fathers of the USA, a distrust of government is considered to be a healthy democratic attribute. The issue of transparency then manifests as, although citizens might be willing to provide any and all private and personal information to private companies and to share it on social media which is, effectively, the world, individuals are reluctant and will resist providing similar information to the government and its agencies.

Notably, in contrast to law enforcement agencies, criminals are early adopters of technology with the ability to deploy technology almost the instant that it becomes available. Unlike publicly funded agencies, criminal enterprises are not subject to intensive processes for tool evaluation, budget appropriation and procurement processes that comply with the regulatory environment. How does law enforcement negate the impact of such reluctance to take advantage of developments in technology that will lead to better protection of the citizenry? Although it is easier said than done, the key to the acquisition and use of contemporary technology is transparency and community consultation. Those government agencies that have successfully introduced new technology and advanced procedures to aid investigations and other public goods have engaged in intensive community engagement processes. Where the introduction of technological advancements have failed, the absence of effective community engagement and leadership is often characteristic of the implementation process.

Mutual legal assistance (MLA)

The brief history of investigations involving digital evidence has been distinctively characterised by the borderless nature of the crime with the possibility of the perpetrator(s), the victim(s), the witness(es) and the evidence all located in different jurisdictions. As technology continues to develop, as it clearly is, the nature of digital investigations is becoming increasingly international, and yet, the methods of requesting and exchanging necessary investigative information remain reliant on traditional, laborious and time-consuming protocols. Central to these traditional protocols is the mutual legal assistance process, which is a process that is generally used for obtaining material that cannot be obtained on a police cooperation basis, particularly for those enquiries that involve coercive processes [5].

The growing internationalisation of criminal investigations together with its consequent growth in MLA requests, investigators are becoming increasingly concerned and frustrated with the international cooperation request process. There are significant challenges including the monitoring of proportionality of outgoing requests, apparent differences of opinion between the requesting and receiving jurisdictions regarding the prioritisation of requests, multiple follow-up requests that draw on resources to respond to the follow-up, differences in language and definitions between requesting and receiving jurisdictions and the disproportionate effort required to action the request in comparison with the penalty that the charges might attract on conviction.

Prior to lodging a formal MLA request, it is recommended that an informal contact is made with the receiving country. The receiving country can advise the requesting country whether or not a request can be executed, the process for making a request, the specific information that is required and the language and format that are to be used. Data preservation, of which timeliness is critical in investigations involving digital evidence, does not normally require a formal MLA request and can be initiated informally. Requests for data preservation can be facilitated through various intermediary organisations such as Interpol.

Documents that provide information on MLA processes can generally be found in most countries and will include contact information for the central authority and, for some countries, general information for making an MLA request. The documents are for broad use and are not usually specific to digital evidence; therefore digital evidence is treated in the same way as other evidence. The UNODC provides a comprehensive manual for requesting states including how to respond to and follow up on incoming requests. The UNODC manual also includes specific information on computer records. The most common information exchange protocols used are those of Interpol, Europol and the Budapest Convention of the Council of Europe.

The most commonly requested information is for IP addresses, social media, Internet access logs and the forensic imaging of devices. However, writing digital evidence requests can be challenging for the requesting agency. The challenges include, when seeking the acquisition of appropriate documents from the requested country, describing the scope of the required evidence and defining the exchange protocols. It is rare for requesters to receive all of the requested information, and sometimes, no information is received.

Usually, when MLA requests are written, they fail to specify the formats, handling, transfer, verification and other parameters that are described in, for example, ISO 17025 accreditation documents. The requesting country is, therefore, leaving it to the receiving country to set the standards for the collection and transfer and evidence. In many countries the national standards do not meet the standards of requesting countries which leaves some question over the integrity of the evidence and therefore its probative value and its weight in any proceedings. It is not difficult to imagine the consequences when presenting evidence derived from unspecified handling, especially in a court that has an expectation of certain standards.

References

[1] P. Kirk, Crime Investigation: Physical Evidence and the Police Laboratory, Interscience Publishers, New York, London, 1953.

[2] Hosting Facts, Internet Stats & Facts for 2019, Retrieved from, https://hostingfacts.com/internet-facts-stats/, 2020.

[3] https://wearesocial.com/blog/2020/01/digital-2020-3-8-billion-people-use-social-media.

[4] Retail Perceptions, The Rise of Webrooming: A Changing Consumer Landscape, Retrieved from, http://www.retailperceptions.com/2014/05/the-rise-of-webrooming/, 2020.

[5] J. James, P. Gladyshev, A survey of mutual legal assistance involving digital evidence, Digit. Evid. 18 (2016) 23–32.

Emerging trends

17

Over the next few years, there are expected to be a number of emerging trends in consumer and business technology that will directly and indirectly impact on the practice and execution of digital evidence. An organisation's ability to address the emerging trends will impact its ongoing effectiveness in meeting its mission. Leaders of the organisational digital evidence capability will be responsible for anticipating the emerging trends and market innovations, the impact that they will have on organisational capability and capacity and to ensure that the capability and capacity of the team are prepared. Anticipation and preparation for emerging trends in digital evidence results from a many faceted approach to leadership including, but not limited to, articulating a vision and a supporting narrative; the ongoing education and training of staff; budget and resources; and buy in from the organisation's executive. A key to successfully meeting emerging trends is to not only look at the challenges that are posed by emerging technologies, but also to look at the opportunities that emerging technologies can provide to meet those evidence challenges.

Several technology and consulting companies invest significant resources, time and effort to anticipate emerging technologies. Some of the predicted broad trends include the following:

- sensing and motion technologies
- augmented human blurring the boundary between the physical and digital worlds
- postclassical computer and communications with quantum computing becoming a practical reality
- digital ecosystems comprising suppliers, customers, trading partners, applications, third-party data service providers and all technologies that support the ecosystem
- advanced artificial intelligence and data analytics, the science applied to the analysis of raw data [1]

Technologies to impact on digital evidence

There are many technologies in various stages of development before they are offered to market. Those trends that are at the peak of development and ready for implementation into business and consumer markets are as follows:

Edge artificial intelligence refers to algorithms that run on local computers or the associated embedded systems. A common Edge AI is the home smart speaker when the 'wake' command is locally stored on the speaker. Edge AI will replace traditional IoT configurations. In current ecosystems, sensors and devices are connected directly via a router to the Internet that provides data to a server, where algorithms then process the data to predict situations concerning the state and the environment of the device.

Strategic Leadership in Digital Evidence. https://doi.org/10.1016/B978-0-12-819618-2.00017-6

Low earth orbit satellite systems will enable the provision of high-speed Internet in places where it is economically unviable to lay optic fibre, such as in emerging markets or sparsely populated regions. Low earth orbit is 500–2000 km above the surface of the earth compared with traditional satellites that orbit around 36,000 km. The attraction for Internet services is the reduced latency (the time taken for data to be transmitted and received and a reply completed) from ~600 milliseconds to speeds approaching those of terrestrial services.

Autonomous driving is perhaps more commonly known as the self-driving car. Substantial research and investment is being undertaken by established motor vehicle manufacturers and technology companies. Reduced latency and improved intelligent systems will improve the viability of autonomous vehicles.

Edge analytics refers to the performance of data analysis at a noncentral point such as at a switch, a peripheral node or a connected device, as found in Internet of Things. Edge analytics configurations enable greater speeds for data processing and response.

Artificial intelligence platform as a service (PaaS) refers to the application of AI in cloud services. Established platform as a service is an environment for building, deploying and maintaining applications and comprises combinations of hardware infrastructure and software solutions. AI PaaS vendors offer pretrained models and algorithms that can solve specific tasks such as the extraction of features, prediction of outcomes and performance of complex calculations.

Biochips are logical devices, or microchips, that are designed to function in a biological environment, such as within a living organism. They can be designed to perform thousands of parallel biochemical reactions and to measure large numbers of biological indicators within an organism.

5G telecommunications is the next generation of telecommunications for mobile digital networks. The network operates on three band spectrums, in which each band spectrum will differ in speed, the ability to penetrate walls and feature extremely low latency. The benefits of 5G include significantly faster data speeds, improved latency, power efficiency, spectral efficiency, high mobility at speed and improved connection density that will support many more connected devices than current LTE systems. This will lead to improved capacity and speed of broadband; a generational improvement in the viability of autonomous vehicles in which vehicles are able to exchange information while on the road; more efficient public infrastructure; remote control of heavy machinery and improved telemedicine with remote recovery, precision surgery and remote surgery; and it will provide a major boost to IoT.

The fifth generation of mobile phone networks is now becoming a reality in many countries. 5G will bring user speeds of 10 gigabits per second (compared with the current up to 35 megabits per second), a 1000-fold increase in system capacity and 100-fold increase in connection density over current LTE and LTE-advanced networks. The advances will impact the specialisation of mobile network forensics, the cross discipline of digital forensics and cellular network analysis that seeks to '… investigate cellular network-facilitated crimes….' Key technologies that accompany the introduction of 5G include Control and User Plane Separation (CUPS) permitting the deployment and use of 5G more efficient for scaling; network functional virtualisation (NFV), a technique that can virtualise an entire class of functions without the need for custom hardware for each function; network slicing that allows portions of the network to be divided for specific customer use cases; and Cellular Internet of Things (CIoT) in which IoT devices connect to the Internet via the mobile network rather than via a router. 5G will support the deployment of new devices and functions including high-speed vehicles and trains, IoT devices, commercial air to ground service and service for light aircraft and helicopters, which will be facilitated by the new and/or enhanced 5G network technologies. These new technologies (CUPS, NFV, network slicing, and CIoT) provide new opportunities for lawful interception and lawful access to location services. The NFV will cause a significant reconfiguration of law enforcement processes, and law enforcement agencies cannot assume that the network infrastructure will be regulated for forensic readiness and will have preestablished points of interception and localization. Network slicing allows network operators to create customised network partitions based on their preferred business models which can include sharing portions of the network with other operators. This allows for multitenancy of the network with multiple options for management of the network. Laws governing mobile network forensics differ between jurisdictions but, in general, require a warrant and privacy protections for safe storage and analysis of acquired evidence. With the anticipated increase in Internet of Things devices, another avenue for warrantless acquisition of mobile network evidence might be available. An IoT device can be a digital witness that can identify, collect, safeguard and communicate mobile network evidence. It might be necessary for evidence obtained from the IoT device to be correlated with evidence collected from the IoT network operator [2].

Graph analytics, also known as network analysis, is driven by social network influencer analysis which is particularly of interest to marketing managers. But it can be applied to other situations, such as detecting financial crimes including money laundering; banking, benefits and insurance fraud; crime prevention; analysis of power grids and other infrastructure; airline routes and supply chain logistics and life sciences research.

Some technologies are rising and potential implementation is in sight:

Immersive workplaces where employees can move frequently throughout the working day and choose the tools they need and the team they need at the time and place they prefer. COVID-19 has accelerated some aspects of this process and it is now closer to being ready for implementation.

Augmented reality cloud is based on augmented reality, the integration of digital information with the physical environment. Developers are able to access apps from a multitude of providers to produce apps that place digital objects in the physical world and allow for multiuser experiences, for example, Pokémon Go. AR cloud allows for the mass adoption of AR technology and could change the way in which information is stored, so that it is accessible on the move (50% of information searches are already conducted 'on the move') and information is available when and where it is needed. To put it another way, the AR cloud will present a 3-D copy of the world, with the possibility of eliminating the need for a personal device.

Decentralised web, which can also be referred to as '*web 3.0*', is favoured by privacy activists and is based on peer-to-peer technology. In some respects, it is a rebellion against the big tech companies that have taken control of citizens' data. Developers working in this space are developing decentralised apps, or 'DApps'. The decentralised web is seen as a replacement to, for example, Google Docs, where every key stroke is sent to Google (an advertising company). Unlike Google Docs however, decentralised web data files are stored in encrypted form on a network of computers that are unable to read the data. The encryption keys never leave the author; therefore the data are solely under the control of the author.

Generative adversarial networks (GANs) represents the development of machine learning that falls within the set of generative models. Generative models are algorithmic architectures that pit two neural networks against each other to produce, or generate, new synthetic content that can pass for real data. They are widely used in image generation, video generation and voice recognition. GANs can learn to mimic any data and can be taught to create images, music, speech and prose. Consequently, they can be used to generate fake media content.

Adaptive machine learning is a further development of traditional machine learning. Traditional machine learning has two phases: (1) the training phase in which data are collected and ingested and (2) the prediction phase in which the data are analysed to reveal insights and make predictions to aid decision-making. The adaptive approach has a single phase that monitors and learns the changes to the input and output values. For example, it can learn from events that may alter the input data behaviour, such as a market, in real time and make data-informed predictions. The adaptive learning systems can handle billions of features across vast datasets and can be applied to fraud detection, financial market trading, market effectiveness and retail effectiveness.

DigitalOps has led to organisations now transitioning to become digital organisations where management, business and operation processes are now data intensive as the data is integrated with, or brought as close as possible to, corporate platforms. Although DigitalOps is not necessarily a challenge from an investigative point of view, there is scope for investigations to make improved use of data to improve investigational outcomes and timeliness.

Decentralised autonomous organisation is an evolution of the traditional organisational structure in which the relationship between an individual and the organisation, or a politician and the citizenry, is defined by a contract. The interactions between people in decentralised autonomous organisations are defined through self-enforcing, open-source protocols. The traditional top-down structure with its layers of management and bureaucracy is absent with all behaviours defined by the code. It can be deployed in a geographically dispersed manner with coworkers located in different countries. All transactions of the company are recorded and maintained on a blockchain and are, therefore, theoretically incorruptible.

Augmented intelligence is a development of artificial intelligence that is designed to enhance human intelligence rather than replace it. It reflects a human-centred partnership of people and artificial intelligence that enhances cognitive performance, including learning, decision-making and new experiences. It has applications to medicine, education and creative fields where human input is intrinsic to the production.

Flying autonomous vehicles are self-explanatory, but some believe that these vehicles might become integrated into the transport fabric before ground-based autonomous vehicles as there are fewer obstacles (i.e., pedestrians and other vehicles) in the air than on the ground.

Transfer learning refers to a research problem in machine learning where knowledge developed while solving one problem can be stored and used to solve a different, but related, problem.

Artificial emotional intelligence is a subdivision of artificial intelligence that measures, understands, simulates and reacts to human emotions. It is also referred to as affective computing, artificial emotional intelligence, emotion recognition, emotion detection technology or even facial coding.

Light cargo delivery drones are largely self-explanatory and will account for an increasing share of deliveries for business to consumer and business to business.

Synthetic data are the production of data that are not obtained by direct measurement. It is used to address specific needs or conditions for which there is a paucity of real data. Synthetic data can be used to develop and test new fraud detection methods.

Knowledge graph is a complex concept in which a given knowledge domain is modelled by subject matter experts with the assistance of machine learning algorithms. The knowledge graph lies on top of existing databases to link all the data together. Knowledge graphs are more pervasive than is immediately apparent as they are employed by the large, well-known technology companies including Facebook, Google and Microsoft to augment search results. An example used by Google is the enhancement of Google's artificial intelligence when answering questions posed to Google Assistant and Google Home. Knowledge graphs can combine disparate silos of data as often appears in large organisations which often results in the generation of multiple versions of knowledge and overlapping initiatives. Knowledge graphs can access and work with structured and unstructured data, a function that is often beyond the capability of other technologies. They are capable of deeper, contextualised searching to locate relevant facts and contextualised answers and provide future proofing of organisational databases for greater reusability of their data.

Personification is the attribution of human characteristics, for example, emotion, to something that is not human, such as an idea or an animal. It can lead to the belief that the nonhuman entity has the ability to act like a human.

Explainable artificial intelligence, or XAI, refers to the techniques in the application of artificial intelligence whereby the results can be understood by human experts, thereby addressing a significant shortfall of current artificial intelligence models.

To meet the digital evidence needs of organisations in the context of the abovementioned emerging trends, solutions are going to be dependent on balancing the interests of multiple parties who have a requirement for the capability, including and especially privacy concerns. Digital evidence is used in multiple forums which can be broadly described as the courtroom, the boardroom and the warroom, and yet it is becoming increasingly expensive, complex and inaccessible. The impacts of these concerns can be mitigated by improving collaboration between industry, government and academia; centralisation and coordination of research, development and administration of capabilities; mechanisms to exchange digital investigation information that align with stakeholder needs and improved availability and coordination of digital investigation knowledge and advanced capabilities [3]. Considerable concern has been expressed in public forums regarding many of the emerging technologies and in particular, government access to the emerging technologies, especially those seen to be 'intelligent'.

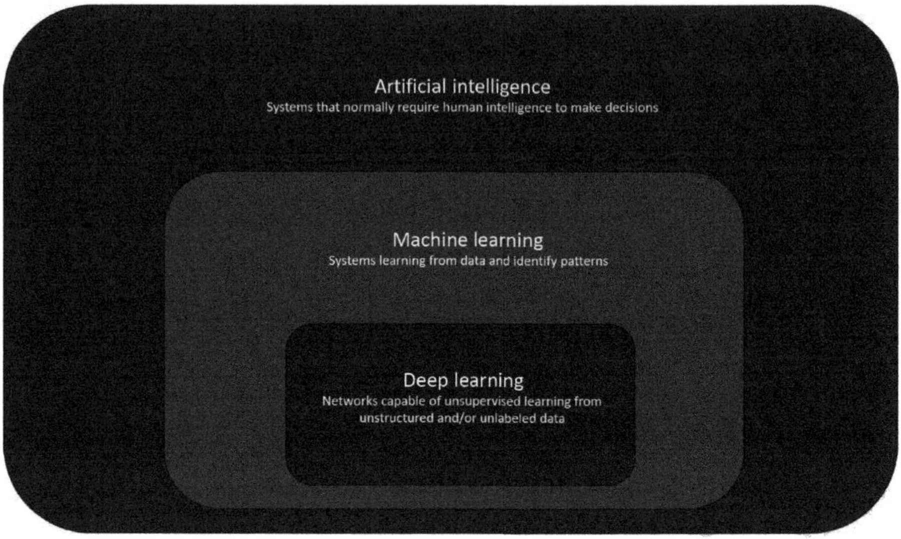

Fig. 17.1 Relationship between artificial intelligence, machine learning, and deep learning.

Some advocates propose that such technologies should be restricted, regulated or subject to strong oversight. While the ethical development, implementation and management of emerging technologies is a public benefit, any ethical framework should not stifle development in the knowledge that private companies, criminal enterprises and potential adversaries are most probably seeking to advance their own technology. An overly restrictive, ethical domestic framework may provide criminal enterprises and adversaries with a competitive advantage over domestic interests and law enforcement agencies (Fig. 17.1).

References

[1] Gartner, Gartner identifies five emerging technology trends with transformational impact, Retrieved from, https://www.gartner.com/en/newsroom/press-releases/2019-29-08-gartner-identifies-five-emerging-technology-trends-with-transformational-impact, August 29, 2019.

[2] F. Sharevski, Towards 5G cellular network forensics, Eurasia J. Inf. Secur. 2018 (2018) 8.

[3] E. Casey, Z. Geradts, B. Nikkel, Editorial: transdisciplinary strategies for digital investigation challenges, Digit. Investig. 25 (2019) 104.

Conclusion

18

The most important requirement of a leader in any field of endeavour is to care for your people, and it is especially true in law enforcement. The work is obviously challenging as it concerns helping people in distress, often at the hands of other people. We do get to see the worst that people can be towards their fellow citizens. The work of the digital evidence experts in dealing with images, video, aural and depraved and violent storytelling is no less disturbing on the video screen than it is in real life.

Moreover, as can probably be assumed, individuals who find themselves interested in and pursuing a career in digital evidence are often a little different to the average person and certainly very different to the typical police officer. The digital evidence expert will be spending all day, every day in front of their video screen, often with head phones on to listen to the audio track, being bombarded by highly disturbing material. The situation must be managed carefully for which there are several workplace features that can mitigate the possibility of severe stress reactions and respond effectively when individuals become affected. Apart from a number of features that are always present in well-led organisations, I recommend some additional, specific features for digital evidence:

- Each person to have a mixed caseload so that they are not performing the same type of case successively. Although there is no such thing as a 'typical' case, an average case will take about 2 weeks. It is not healthy for a person to be working on, for example, successive child abuse cases for an extended period of time.
- Team members should not work alone but work in an open space. Working in a team environment not only engenders better communication (digital evidence practitioners can need encouragement to communicate) but also enables team members to look out for each other. Viewing child abuse or violent extremism material when alone is an unhealthy situation.
- Team members participate in a formal mental health program at regular intervals, for example, twice a year. A good psychologist, who can build rapport with the team members, will be able to identify when a person is struggling. The program should include plans for supporting and managing an individual when they are experiencing the 'wobbles'.
- A good training program that keeps people up to date with the latest advances in technology and digital evidence concepts. I set aside 4 weeks per year per individual which comprised a mixture of whole team training, specific training and project work that targeted to each individual's interest and that addressed a need or emerging technology issue for the team.
- An annual event over 2 days, especially for teams that are geographically dispersed, where each individual presents a 15-minute paper on a relevant topic of their choosing, often the result of a project that they have been working on through the preceding 12 months.

Above all, not only does a leader need to ensure that the mechanics, processes and procedures are all in place, but also I cannot overstate the importance of emotionally intelligent leadership, especially for groups of experts. To paraphrase James Comey, we are all born with some, but it is something that we all can work on [1].

Strategic Leadership in Digital Evidence. https://doi.org/10.1016/B978-0-12-819618-2.00018-8

This book is a reflection of my journey in digital evidence, informed in part by my experiences before entering the field and with a healthy dose of hindsight. Many of the things that I tried worked, and many things did not. I hope that, as you begin your journey in this incredibly sometimes overwhelmingly, fascinating, field, this book provides you with some guidance and a base of information and experience to keep pushing the field forward. If I can offer two pieces of advice: (1) keep listening to people around you, above, below and to the side as technology keeps evolving so fast that it will be hard to keep up, and (2) take care and support the examiners and the pracititoners as they will know more about the field than anyone else around, they love the field and they want the team to be successful.

Reference

[1] J. Comey, A Higher Loyalty: Truth, Lies, and Leadership, Published by Flatiron Books, New York, 2018.

Index

Note: Page numbers followed by *f* indicate figures and *t* indicate tables.

9780128196182